Kissing Kibo:

Trekking to the Summit of Mount Kilimanjaro via the Lemosho Route

Kissing Kibo:

Trekking to the Summit of Mount Kilimanjaro via the Lemosho Route

SHEREE MARSHALL

iUniverse, Inc.
Bloomington

Kissing Kibo: Trekking to the Summit of Mount Kilimanjaro
The Lemosho Route

iUniverse books may be ordered through booksellers or by contacting:

iUniverse
1663 Liberty Drive
Bloomington, IN 47403

www.iuniverse.com
1-800-Authors (1-800-288-4677)

Because of the dynamic nature of the Internet, any Web addresses or links contained in this book may have changed since publication and may no longer be valid. The views expressed in this work are solely those of the author and do not necessarily reflect the views of the publisher, and the publisher hereby disclaims any responsibility for them.

ISBN: 978-1-4502-4024-6 (sc)
ISBN: 978-1-4502-4025-3 (ebook)

Printed in the United States of America

iUniverse rev. date: 4/12/2011

For my nephew
Nehemiah Marshall Jackson

In honor and in loving memory of my parents

Mr. Charles Marshall
1934–1997

and

Mrs. Runell Marshall
1940–2002

ACKNOWLEDGEMENTS

I would like to thank the following people for their written comments on earlier versions of the manuscript: Linda Danavall, MPH; Kimberly Moore Daniel, EdD; Carla Lee, MA; Serigne Ndiaye, PhD; Charlene Sanders, RD, MPH and Laura Whitfield, PMP. Thanks are also extended to *The Reading Group* (Arthur, Cathy, Lynne, Paul, and Tom), a terrific group of friends who provided inspiration through verbal comments, late-night laughs, delicious meals, and jovial digressions; the very things that kept me writing.

CONTENTS

Tanzania

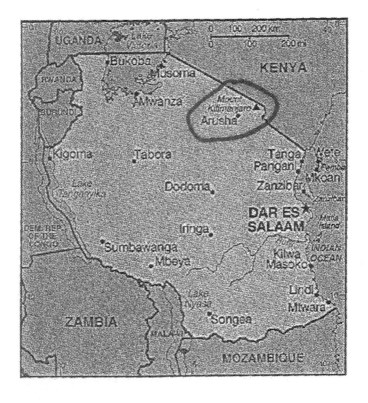

PREFACE

When I first began thinking seriously about trekking Mount Kilimanjaro, I read about the history, flora, fauna, and geology of the mountain. I watched DVD documentaries and read about those who had climbed to the top of Mount Kilimanjaro. I also talked to and e-mailed people who had attempted to summit Mount Kilimanjaro. However, I found that in one way or another, all these sources were limited. Most documentaries featured experienced mountaineers who were in top-notch physical condition and who had climbed other mountains besides Mount Kilimanjaro. The documentaries did not indicate that the climb could be made by ordinary people who were not avid outdoorsmen. Most of the books were based on treks that had occurred more than ten years ago. Thus, much of the written information was outdated, and a great deal had changed on the mountain.

There have been two major changes in particular: more routes to the top and a greater focus on environmental stewardship. Previous books do not account for these. Additionally, most of the books consisted of accounts that were based on trekking the Marangu route, which is the easiest and most common of all routes. I found only one book that was relatively up to date and recounted a person's experience climbing the Umbwe route, which is considerably more difficult. However, it had little information on actual preparation for the climb, as it was basically the climber's unedited diary. While talking with people offered valuable insight, their recollections tended to be spotty, and not one of the people with whom I spoke had actually made it to the top of Mount

Kilimanjaro. My e-mails requesting information on the climb were either unanswered or received a minimal response at best.

With this in mind, I set out to write a book that would fill what I perceived as a gap in the literature: an updated account of the trekking experience of an ordinary person summiting Mount Kilimanjaro via one of the least traveled and more challenging routes, the Lemosho route. At the same time, the book will share information with the reader about ways he or she can best prepare for this awesome adventure on the road less traveled. This is the spirit in which I share my journey and this guide with you.

Chapter 1:   Introduction

The continent of Africa conjures up many thoughts of exotic, unique, and exciting adventures; nothing, however, epitomizes and kindles this excitement like Mount Kilimanjaro. From novels like *The Snows of Kilimanjaro,* written by Ernest Hemmingway, and *Kilimanjaro with Passion*, by Alan Sawaya to jazz tunes such as "Filles de Kilimanjaro," composed by Miles Davis, people have been compelled to memorialize this great work of nature. At 19,340 (5,895m) feet above sea level, Mount Kilimanjaro is the tallest freestanding mountain in the world, and the world's tallest volcano. While there are other mountains that are higher, no other is freestanding, which means that the base of the mountain starts at sea level and is not part of a mountain range. As one of seven continental high points, it is the highest peak and the only permanently snow-capped mountain on the continent of Africa. Most commonly known as Kilimanjaro (Mountain of Greatness), the mountain goes by other names as well: Oldoinyo Oibor (white mountain, in Masai), Kilma Njaro (shining mountain, in Swahili), and Kibo (used by locals).

Although it has not erupted in several millennia, Kilimanjaro is actually a giant stratovolcano that consists of three cones, creating three volcanic summits (Mawenzi, Shira, and Kibo) (Poindexter 1998). Kibo is in the center of the two cones: Mawenzi is located to the east of Kibo, and Shira is located to the west. At the rim of Mount Kilimanjaro's summit is a one-and-one-half mile crater that is roughly 1,000 feet (305m) deep [1].

---

1   Living Africa, "The Land: Mount Kilimanjaro," http://library.thinkquest.org/16645/the land/mount_kilimanjaro.shtml.

For most people around the globe, Mount Kilimanjaro is simply a figment of their imagination—a mystic mountain that few ever ascend. Then there are those of us who will ascend to the very top, as did the indigenous people of the region and European adventure seekers nearly three hundred years ago. Yearly, about 30,000 aspiring climbers attempt to reach the summit; of this number, only 40 percent ever do. For eight or nine people each year, this attempt is fatal[2] .

To talk about Mount Kilimanjaro as having been "discovered" is like talking about man discovering the Moon. There is no such thing. What we do know about man's interaction with this formidable mountain is that it has been the source of awe and spiritual connection for several millennia. There is a great deal of rumor and folklore surrounding Mount Kilimanjaro, such as the belief that Queen Victoria gave the massive peak as a birthday gift to her cousin Kaiser Wilhelm, making it the providence of Tanzania rather than Kenya. Obviously, the mountain was never owned by Queen Victoria, or anyone else for that matter. How does an individual claim ownership of a natural wonder? Quite simply, you cannot.

Thanks to research conducted over the past hundred years or so, we do know a bit about the history of those who ascended this majestic mountain. One of the first Europeans to ascend the mountain was a German-Swedish missionary by the name of Johannes Rebmann (Stedman 2006). Rebmann told of his experiences not only encountering the mountain but encountering those who lived near it and flourished at its foothills. He was the first to note that the people of the Wachagga (or the Chagga, as they are sometimes called by the locals) tribe who lived in the surrounding villages were indeed familiar with the mountain. Thereafter, other missionaries visited Kilimanjaro for the express purpose of "civilizing" and proselytizing to its inhabitants.

On the heels of the missionaries came the mountaineers. These were Europeans who, during the mid-nineteenth century, went to conquer the mountain. Among those making attempts during this time were English geologist Richard Thornton, Hanoverian naturalist Claus von der Decken, and Charles New, a London-born missionary with the United Methodist Church (Stedman 2006). None of these men reached

---

2   Climb Mt. Kilimanjaro, "Mt. Kilimanjaro-How Dangerous Is It Really?," http://www.mtkilimanjarologue.com/planning/random/mt-kilimanjaro-how-dangerous-is-it.

the summit. These earlier adventure-seekers were then followed by others who were more concerned with colonizing the surrounding region than they were with conquering Mt. Kilimanjaro. When colonizers became interested in the mountain during the late 1800s, it was a German professor, Hans Meyer, who discovered something that other mountaineers apparently had never thought of: it would be impossible to reach Kibo, the summit of Mount Kilimanjaro, without a local guide who was intimately familiar with the mountain's geography and the terrain.

Yohani Kinyala Lauwo, known as Kinyala by the people of the local Marangu village, was the first man known to have climbed Mount Kilimanjaro. Kinyala had spent his childhood and adolescence romping through the slopes of Kilimanjaro exploring the mountain forest that supplied his community with honey, timber, medicine, and colobus monkey hides. As a member of the Wachagga tribe, Kinyala and other Wachagga had hunted the surrounding forest of Mount Kilimanjaro for elephants to get ivory which they then sold to Swahili traders from the coast. He was only eighteen years old when he led Hans Meyer to the highest point of Africa on October 5, 1889[3]. He was personally chosen by the Wachagga chief, Mangi, to make Han Meyer's dream come true: to be the first European to summit Mount Kilimanjaro. In 1989, the German government, as a way of thanking Lauwo, built him a house to commemorate the one hundredth anniversary of the climb. To this day, the Wachagga still serve as the primary guides on Mount Kilimanjaro, while Germans make up the majority of the trekkers. How appropriate that my trekking guide, who is Wachagga, opened his introduction to our expedition with the words, "We are here to make your dream come true." All these years later, the Wachagga are still making the dreams of Europeans and other adventure-seekers across the globe come true!

Meyer also realized that a major impediment to reaching the summit was the lack of food and other supplies needed for survival. Thus, it was also clear to him that he would need not only a guide but other people fit enough to carry his food and equipment while he ascended the mountain. Therefore, he employed *porters*, local persons who are acclimated to the terrain, to ascend the mountain with him, while

---

3   Nichole Smaglick, "The Old Man of Mt. Kilimanjaro"http://www.ntz.info/gen/n02213.html.

carrying his edibles and other camping equipment. He also created stations where he could eat and refuel at various points along his journey up the mountain. These stations later came to be known as *camps*. Today, all three of these aspects of trekking are in place: guides, porters, and camps. In fact, it is now mandatory (i.e., required by Tanzanian law) that each trekker employ a licensed mountain guide, and almost no trekker ascends without porters.

The Germans' interest in colonizing Kilimanjaro, while met with unrest and brute force by the inhabitants of Moshi, ironically served to connect succeeding generations of Germans to the Moshi region and to the magnificent mountain. While the Wachagga people were content to live in harmony with this mysterious mountain and rely on it for their spiritual worship and physical sustenance, European explorers were more interested in exploring the geography of the mountain and exploiting the people and land at its base. One positive result of the European adventurers' selfish goals was that it brought notoriety to Mount Kilimanjaro and generated worldwide excitement about this expansive land, drawing attention to this miracle of creation in our midst. Now, in the twenty-first century, we have come full circle. The descendents of the first European explorers, the native Wachagga, and others who simply want to encounter the awe and beauty of the legendary mountain are free to experience Kilimanjaro in their own personal way. Symbolic of this renewed interest, the name given to Kibo in 1918 has been changed from Kaiser-Wilhelm-Spitze, to Uhuru Peak. Uhuru, in Swahili, means "freedom."

Who Is This Book Written For?

This book is an informal travel guide to assist you in preparing for your trek to the top of Mount Kilimanjaro. It is written for the ordinary person who has an extraordinary desire. If you are a single woman with an adventurous spirit, this book is for you. If you are like me, a woman who grew up in suburban America and has never hiked or camped, yet has an affinity for the outdoors, this book is for you. If you are a novice climber, regardless of your gender, you will find this book useful as you are planning your ascent of one of the world's most awe-inspiring peaks using the road less traveled: the Lemosho route.

Who Is This Book Not Written For?

This book is neither a memoir nor an official travel guide. The well-seasoned mountaineer may find it relentlessly boring, and the history buff might well look elsewhere. This book is not written to entertain or offer factual information not found elsewhere; rather it is simply written to inform and inspire.

How My Odyssey Began

I began dreaming of climbing Mount Kilimanjaro many years before I mustered up the guts to actually climb. I was well into the second decade of my profession as a behavioral scientist and professor, I had no children (although I was pondering the idea of adopting), and I was in a committed relationship (with no plans to wed). My mother died of breast cancer at age fifty-nine and my father died of heart disease at age sixty-three. Having lost both parents at a relatively young age, I began to think that I had more good days behind me than in front of me. At this point in my life, I felt that if I wanted to be adventurous and travel, I'd better learn to do things by myself. So I set out to plan a trip of a lifetime.

It was an opportunity to be alone, with me. I had consciously intended to wrestle with issues that had long plagued me: self-doubt, depression, remorse, and regret. There was one question in particular that I really wanted an answer to: whether I had let my mother, who had died of cancer a few years earlier, down during the time when we (my sister, she, and I) were fighting for her life. Then there was the issue of where was my life going. What did I really want out of life? I wanted to wrestle with these issues and questions alone, with the help of Mother Nature. After a failed marriage, I had resigned to the fact that at the age of forty-five I'd join the ranks of millions of other middle-aged African American women I knew, who after divorce never remarried and never bore children. This, I reasoned, would be my first of many forays into going at it alone.

There was yet another factor in all this. It was something I had reflected on for many years: All my life, men had provided for me and women had nurtured me. I don't mean "provided" in the sense that men bought things for me that I otherwise could not have bought for myself; however, beginning with my father, the men in my life always provided a sense of security and ensured my material wellbeing. Women, on the other hand, provided me with solace. Women consoled me. The women in my life helped me to think about the path forward. This is a major reason why I miss my mother so terribly. I wanted to understand why this gender pattern existed in my life. So as you can see, I started my climb with lots of issues.

The ascent would be eight days of the hardest physical activity I had done in my entire life. I set out, alone, to climb Africa's highest peak. Two days before leaving for Africa, I did not engage in any strenuous activity, but rather enjoyed the company of two good friends. We had dinner at one of our favorite Thai restaurants in Atlanta. The following evening I had dinner with my sister and her family. They wished me well and said their good-byes. I do not think they thought that I'd return, because they felt compelled to go around the table and say how much they loved me, and then my sister gave me a beautiful bouquet of yellow roses—the same kind we used to give my mother on Mother's Day. After dinner, I said a heartfelt good-bye, asked them not to worry about me, and hurried home to pack the last of my belongings. I never slept. Instead, I kept packing right up until 3:00 a.m. on Sunday, July 20, 2008. At 3:00 a.m., I said good-bye to my pooch, Vince, and was driven to the airport by my boyfriend, Tom. We arrived at the airport around 4:00 a.m., with more than enough time to check in and board my 5:40 a.m. flight. At the airport, Tom and I joked around at the terminal, reminisced about the trip that we'd taken to Africa just a couple of years earlier, and took pictures before I bid him a tearful farewell and headed out on my twenty-three-hour journey to the other side of the world for an adventure with Mother Nature—an experience that I felt was long overdue.

CHAPTER 2: DAILY TREKKING LOG, MY JOURNEY

I arrived at Kilimanjaro National Airport one week before I was scheduled to take the trek. Upon my arrival, there was a car waiting to take me to my accommodation, the Ngurdoto Mountain Lodge, a beautiful, rustic building set amidst coffee plantations. For the next five days, I would spend time visiting the town of Arusha, where I ate local foods, shopped at the fresh fruit and vegetable markets, and toured the Arusha National Park and Wildlife Center. Arriving in the city well before my scheduled trek gave me an opportunity to acclimatize before ascending to much higher elevations. Acclimatization days are critical, given that I had flown in from such a low altitude.

The nondescript Kilimanjaro International Airport where my flight landed and I was met by a representative from the Kilisummit Safari and Adventure trekking company.

Fig. 2.1. Ngurdoto Lodge where I stayed five days preceding my trek.

Fig. 2.2. Me in front of the public library in Arusha, Tanzania.

Fig. 2.3. Alligators in the Arusha National Park.

On the fourth day of my stay, the local trekking guide, Nickson Moshi, and his counterpart from the United States, Natalie Latzka, came to my suite to meet with me to discuss the upcoming trek. When Nickson and Natalie entered my suite, they were both very cordial and did not look at all like I had imagined. Nickson is a muscular, medium-built, richly dark middle-aged man who appears younger than his years. He has a round, plump, friendly face with small, dark eyes and pronounced cheekbones. Natalie is a tall, stocky, Scandinavian-looking woman with blond hair and blue eyes. She has that matter-of-fact, no-nonsense way of speaking so characteristic of Midwesterners.

Natalie approached me with a bit of curiosity. She raised her eyebrows and seemed to want to ask, "So, what brings you here?" But instead she said, "Nice to meet you" as she held out her hand. Nickson, on the other hand, seemed to go out of his way to be dispassionate. He spoke of his experience leading treks and then went on to discuss other perfunctory issues. I asked about the weather on the mountain and how I would choose the appropriate clothes to wear. In a bland but not rude manner, he stated, "I will tell you what to wear, what time to get up, and which way to go." At any other time in my life, I would have had a serious problem with anyone speaking to me in such a dictatorial way. This time, I simply said, "I see." Afterward, I thanked Nickson and Natalie for coming to my room and speaking with me about the trek. I walked them to the door and told them that I would be sure to be in the lobby promptly tomorrow morning.

On the day that we were scheduled to begin our trek, I awoke completely rested. I felt exuberant as I packed my belongings. After a hot cup of tea, I lugged my gear from my second-floor suite to the lobby so that it could be retrieved and placed in the van by the hotel staff. I then went to the restaurant in the lodge to have breakfast. While eating alone, I glanced over at two women eating at the table just in front of me. Among all the dark African faces and bodies that were all elaborately adorned in vibrant, deep-colored cloths and headdresses, the two women stood out. They were very nicely dressed European American women in some of the best hiking getups I'd seen. Both were eating while gazing out the window, looking contemplative and saying very little to each other. I also noticed that they each had really nice trekking poles leaning on the side of the table. Given their appearance, I surmised that these were probably my Colorado trekking partners, so I got up from the table and went over to introduce myself.

"Hi, are you by any chance here for the Mount Kilimanjaro hike with Nickson."

"Yes," they said, in unison.

"I am too." I replied. "I think we're in the same party."

"Really?" the older of the two responded. "What's your name?"

"Sheree. And yours."

"I'm Karen, and this is my daughter, Mori" she said, as she pointed towards the young woman seated at the table with her.

We then shook hands and exchanged banal introductions. Afterward, I went back to my table and gathered a few croissants to take with me on the drive to the start of the trek. An hour or so later, Nickson formally introduced us to each other. We took pictures and then proceeded to the van that would take us to the start of the Lemosho route.

Fig. 2.4. Expedition seated in the lobby of the Ngurdoto Lodge: From left to right, me, Nickson, Karen, and Mori.

The following excerpts are from the diary that I kept while on the mountain. (For an actual page from my diary, see appendix B.) Generally, I wrote in my log at the end of each day. My log reflects this, in that on some days I posted long notes, while on other days my notes were brief. You'll also notice that in some cases the notes are written in past tense while in other instances they are written in the present. That is because in some cases, I wrote in my journal the following day because I was too tired to pen my thoughts.

Day 1

July 27, 2008
The first day of the trek began with everyone congregating near the check-in point. There were about fifty porters hovering around the trekkers hoping to get a job carrying the mountain gear. As the porters were assembling, our party was introduced to two people who would

become indispensible. We met Dastan, the assistant guide and the gentleman who would serve as our cook. Shortly afterward, our party formed a line in front of a small enclosed wooden shed that had only enough room for one person. The man inside the wooden shed asked to see a passport and then asked each trekker to sign a log book. Trekkers are required to write their name, age, citizenship, and address in a thick note tablet containing entries that date back several years.

After signing the log book, the two women in my party, the guide, the cook, and I packed into an SUV that looked like it had seen better days. We proceeded on a thirty-minute drive to the Londrossi Gate, the side of the forest where the Lemosho route begins. The road was extremely rocky. In fact, rather than a road, it was more like a series of potholes strung together with a ribbon of hard-packed earth. The bounces were dizzying, and I was getting sick from all of the shaking back and forth. It was drizzling rain, and the SUV kept getting stuck in mud puddles. At one point, the other two women and I got out of the SUV and watched helplessly as the guide and cook dislodged the SUV from the mud. On the way to the beginning of the route, we passed local people tending potato and carrot crops that were growing in abundance at the base of the mountain. We stopped briefly at the hut in front of the Londrossi Gate so that our guide could pay the park fees before we finally reached the beginning of the Lemosho Route. By this time, the rain had stopped. As I looked up, all I could see was an unbroken canopy of trees from every angle. We were nestled deep in the middle of the rain forest. It was here where we would begin our trek.

There was another couple ahead of us preparing to embark. They were giving sunglasses to all their porters to wear when they got above the tree line, where the sun would be intense. As I stood watching, I wished I had thought to bring a gift item to distribute to our crew. Before starting the trek, we were provided a small lunch consisting of fresh tomatoes and papayas, butter and cheese sandwiches, and boiled eggs. The papaya and tomatoes were excellent. I must admit, though, that the butter and cheese sandwich was not my favorite. I couldn't imagine consuming chunks of butter and cheese together, let alone with boiled eggs! I reached into my bag and pulled out the croissant that I had saved from the hotel breakfast and ate it.

After lunch, the porters packed the table where we'd eaten, along with our duffle bags, tents, and other assorted items, headed up the incline, and disappeared into the forest. Not long afterward, our trekking party followed behind them in single file. The assistant guide was in front of the group, I was behind him, fellow trekker Karen was behind me, her daughter, Mori, behind her and then Nickson, the guide. The trek began in the rainforest at about 6,890 feet. Starting out, we were completely enveloped by the lush, green forest. I found myself completely absorbed by my surroundings and wanting to inspect every plant, leaf, moss and creature that peered through the thicket. Everything in the forest seemed so full of life. When I looked up all I could see was an integument of green with an occasional glimpse of the bright sun. It was as if Nature was giving me a big hug!

As we moved through the forest, Nickson and Dastan pointed out the various plant species, such as the *Impatiens* species (e.g., the *kilimanjaro* and *pseudoviola*) and the giant trees, such as the camphor, podocarpus, and hagenia. By the end of the day, we had gone up to about 10,000 feet, although it really didn't feel as though we had ascended much at all. We made camp at the first campground, called Mti Mkubwa (Big Tree Camp). This camp site is small, and there were about twenty other trekkers making camp at the same time. The porters had already assembled my tent, and I began placing my belongings inside. It was dusk, but it would soon turn pitch dark. We had a small meal by candlelight before retiring. During the night, the temperature was moderate, around 76 degrees Fahrenheit, and surprisingly warm in my tent. I was quite comfortable throughout the night. The main event was getting used to the strange noises in the night—including colobus monkeys (which tend to be very small) jumping from one tent to another. One monkey seemed to be using the top of my tent as a trampoline. Despite this commotion, I slept very well.

Fig. 2.5. Nickson, the guide (standing) and Dastan, the assistant guide.

Fig. 2.6. Me in the rainforest on the first day of the trek.

Day 2

July 28, 2008

We started the trek at 8:00 a.m. and ended at 3:00 p.m., walking the seven hours with a short (45-minute) break. During the break, we had lunch on a flat part of the mountain that provided stellar vistas. Here we were treated to a splendid meal consisting of baked potatoes, pasta, squash, and fish. It was a lovely feeling, as if time were standing still, the wind blowing at my back and the sun beaming down on my face. We spent the first part of the day trekking through the forest and ended at the point where we reached heath and moorland. It was interesting to see the large trees that were completely covered with moss. (I later found out that these mosses are called *bearded lichen*). The moss so completely covers the leaves that it gives the impression that the trees themselves are made of moss. During our trek, we passed through areas of very thin trails with lots of tall grass. We ended the day at Shira I/ Fischer camp.

Fig. 2.7. Me standing in front of mountain vistas at 12,000 feet.

Fig. 2.8. The lunchtime meal served on Day 2: potatoes, Tilapia fish, pasta and squash.

Day 3

July 29, 2008

Left Shira I at 8:30 a.m. and trekked northwest to Shira II Camp. The walk was fairly flat, with a few streams along the way. The streams often fed the huge *senecios*, also known as *the giant* or *tree groundsel,* growing along their borders. Senecios are large indigenous trees that tend to grow along the border of streams and in damper, more sheltered parts of the mountain. It was amazing to see these hundred-foot trees towering over all the other vegetation in the moorland. We hiked for five and a half hours today, from 8:30 a.m. until 2:00 p.m. There was plenty of time for contemplation and meditation. Afterward, we had a hot lunch consisting of vegetables, toast, pasta, and sauce with vegetables. We also had soup. The soup was very creamy and appeared to be canned soup spruced up with spices and fresh vegetables.

We are at an altitude of 12,600 feet. Tomorrow, we ascend to an altitude of 15,000 feet, and we have been told that it will be a long trek, lasting about seven hours. Today, as always, I was humbled by the porters' lot, having to carry all of our equipment and supplies (including cooking utensils and even a propane tank!) up the mountain. At the same time, I and the others in our group are traveling empty-handed with our measly ten-pound backpacks, lagging behind the porters while complaining of the journey that lay ahead.

Today was a good day. I had no symptoms of mountain sickness and am really thankful for that. I have been taking Diamox (for altitude sickness) for the past five days and apparently it is working. I became a bit winded on one part of the trek this afternoon, when we were scaling rocks. The rest of the trail was fairly easy—just lots of walking. As I write, I am a bit nervous, because I see a pack of jackals just over the horizon, perhaps a few hundred feet from my tent. Nickson has told us not to worry, because the jackals mainly eat vegetables and small animals. They are not interested in human flesh. As I nestle into my sleeping bag, I silently wonder whether jackals can differentiate between a small animal and a small bundle of human flesh.

Fig. 2.9. Me resting on a boulder and enjoying the mountain vistas. I have a scarf wrapped around my head to stay cool.

Day 4

July 30, 2008

It's 11:00 p.m., and I have just awakened. I have been sleeping since 7:00 p.m. I was really tired when I arrived here at the Shira II camp site this afternoon. It was a hard hike for me. I came down with acute mountain sickness (AMS) right as we reached an altitude of about 14,600 feet. From that point on, walking became difficult and my head began to hurt. I also experienced shortness of breath. The symptoms throughout the day were mainly tiredness and headache. I took a couple of Tylenol and kept walking. At one point during the hike, Dastan and I took a break to rest. As I sat on this huge boulder trying to catch my breath and hoping not to faint, I could barely sit upright because of excruciating head pain and my queasy stomach. At this point, Dastan, with this innocent look of pity on his face, reached into his coat pocket and handed me a twisted cheese and butter sandwich that he had had stuffed in his jacket three hours earlier. Although I realized he was trying so hard to be nice, it seemed to me like a cruel joke. I looked at the barely recognizable sandwich and shook my head to indicate the word "no." I did not have the energy to speak.

Finally, by the grace of God, after walking almost five hours, I made it to an altitude of 15,000 feet. Rather than continuing on the route from Barafu Camp to Baranco Camp, we are camping out here at Shira II today. We've been told that we'll wake up mid-morning tomorrow (here on the mountain that means around 9:30 a.m.), pack our belongings, and head for the next camp, which I understand is only a ninety-minute hike of about one and a half miles. Nickson is allowing us to sleep in tomorrow to assist us with acclimatization. Today we hiked four and a half hours, from 8:30 a.m. until 1:00 p.m.

Here at the camp, the wind is blowing my tent ferociously. It feels as though I'm in the middle of a major windstorm. The tent is rocking back and forth. We are in somewhat of a valley and there is an ominous-looking cloud forming above us. I am a bit scared, because I fear that a major storm is approaching. Nickson says it's always very windy at this point on the mountain. This was very reassuring. I'm really glad that I have a warm sleeping bag. It's very toasty. I have been thinking about

Tom and my family a lot today, hoping they're okay. I've been especially praying that my nephew Nehemiah is doing well.

Today, Dastan became my personal trekking guide. Because my pace became so much slower than the two other women in my trekking group, Dastan stayed behind to walk with me. Karen and her daughter ascended the mountain at a brisk pace and did not seem to be bothered by altitude sickness. This may be because they both live at fairly high altitudes in Colorado and have both ascended to heights of 14,000 feet. I suspect that they are pretty well acclimatized to this altitude. I, on the other hand, living at 750 feet above sea level and rarely ascending above 2,000 feet, am having a much harder time adjusting.

I feel much better now, after having a hot meal and rest. I think I'll be okay to hike an hour or so tomorrow and then to the summit afterwards. My fingernails are totally black from all the dusty volcanic soil that gets into your nose and under your fingernails. Although my hair is tightly braided, I'm sure it is filthy! I have decided that after arriving back at the lodge, the first thing I'll do is take a long, hot bath!

On today's hike, Dastan, was superb. Every now and then he would look back and say "Polepole" (Swahili for "slowly") and then ask, "Are you okay, daughter?" Within Wachagga culture, the word "daughter" is used to address middle-aged women.

"Yes," I'd say, and we'd keep walking.

Other times he'd say, "Are you drinking? Let's stop. Drink-ed" (with an emphasis on the 'ed'), then we'd stop and I'd take a sip from my hydration pack. It's amazing how a person can be all that you need at the very time you need him. I am very grateful! I have decided that I'll give him the biggest tip that I can reasonably afford.

On the way up, Dastan and I passed a woman who seemed to be suffering from severe mountain sickness and was barely able to walk. She and a man were being taken down the mountain. The man, I was told, was suffering from asthma and having difficulty breathing. My resting pulse rate is now somewhere between 110 and 123. That's okay—I think—although it is higher than my normal resting rate of 72.

Day 5

July 31, 2008

It's 11:30 a.m. on Thursday, July 31. We've just arrived at Arrow-Glacier Camp after leaving Lava Tower Camp at around 9:30 a.m. It was an uphill hike the entire way. This camp site is much more remote and seems more littered than the others. The porters are busy scurrying around getting things prepared for lunch. I feel a bit tired, with a slight striking pain on the right side of my head, but other than that, I am okay. This is the fifth day of the trek. My fingernails are still black with dust and dirt from the volcanic rock. My face is dusty and so is my hair. My clothes are the same. It is a clear, pretty, sunny day. We are just above the clouds. It seems as if we can almost touch the snow on the side of the mountain. It's gotten too hot for my long underwear, so I'm going to take one pair off and try to relax at the camp. Hopefully, I'll be able to retire early and prepare for the next day's journey. Tomorrow, we will ascend 2,000 feet to an altitude of 18,000.

It's 3:09 p.m. I am retiring in my tent and contemplating, journaling under the marvelous African sun. The sky is so clear. The glaciers on the mountain are pristine, cascading down the sides of the mountain like frosting overrun on a chocolate cake. It's simply breathtaking. Although there is much criticism heaped on the Europeans for claiming they "discovered" Mount Kilimanjaro, and that they trekked to the top before Africans did, I think they should be given every bit of credit for exposing this marvel to the rest of the world, especially the Western world. [*I did not rest well at Arrow Camp, because this afternoon, at about 4:30 p.m., an expedition from Great Britain arrived, and they were very noisy. There was also a young woman in their group who drank heavily and then stayed up vomiting all night*].

Day 6

August 1, 2008 (still at Arrow-Glacier Camp)

I awoke around 6:30 a.m. After getting dressed, the trekking party assembled at the table in the main tent and had breakfast, which consisted of a porridge, coffee, tea, and cookies. I had been up all night. Between the drunken stupor of some of the Brits, the gushing heaving and vomiting of another British trekker, and the upset stomach that I acquired shortly after dinner, it was impossible to sleep. I had no idea what the day would bring: the wretched wear-and-tear to my body as my stamina, endurance, and human spirit were all tested. We set out at about 7:30 a.m. I felt extremely cold. The temperature was about 10 degrees Fahrenheit. I started out wearing my down jacket, but had to shed it almost immediately because I was getting too warm while walking. We began trekking north and upward with the goal of reaching an altitude of 18,000 feet. From the outset, I was behind the other two women in my trekking party. So the assistant guide had the task of trekking with me at a much slower pace. Onward we went. As we walked, I became sicker and sicker. My head felt light as we trudged on. I tried, luckily with success, to hold back the urge to vomit. I knew that if I began vomiting, I wouldn't stop, and that that would be a sure sign that I was moving from mild acute mountain sickness (AMS) into moderate AMS, which is where high-altitude cerebral edema (HACE) and high-altitude pulmonary edema (HAPE) gain their foothold. As we moved forward, every step seemed to get harder and harder. I kept looking forward and told myself not to look down, behind, or to the sides, just straight ahead. This seemed to help with my AMS symptoms, which by now were an excruciating headache, dizziness, and an upset stomach. The ground appeared to be spinning. I'd began experiencing many of these symptoms while ascending 2,000 feet in altitude in less than five hours!

We trekked on, with me following behind the guide. With each step we took, my admiration of the guide grew. He traversed the landscape with such ease, strength, and agility. I began to look to him for inner strength.

"Do you think I can make it?" I asked.

"Yes, daughter, you will make it."

"Okay," I said. "Okay."

As I trudged on, I tried to remove all negative thoughts, like the ones I'd left behind in Atlanta: "You're going to die on that mountain," or "I'm afraid you'll end up in a coma." These thoughts kept trying to force themselves into my consciousness, but I would not let them take hold. I kept moving and chanting the phrase *"The race goes not to the swift or strongest, but to him that endures."* Then I thought about my mom. She had tried to endure. Was it me who gave up?

Then there were times when I would try not to think at all, like when we were scaling rocks and boulders on the side of the mountain. At 18,000 feet, in very thin air, we had to hold on to each rock and climb across several steep ledges, sometimes on my hands and knees, always one hand holding firmly to a rock and the other hand holding desperately to the hand of the assistant guide, Dastan, who kept saying, "Here, hold my hand." At one point, I let go of Dastan's hand to grasp a boulder just above me. At the same time, I took a step onto the next rock with my left foot, while my right foot was resting on another. When the rock on which my right foot was resting slipped, I lost my purchase on the boulder immediately above me. In a flash, the guide quickly grabbed my left hand. I did not look back. I did not need to in order to know that if I had fallen, it would have been a long way down! From that point on, every time the guide offered his outstretched hand, I held on to it without fail.

As I scrambled on, there were no thoughts in my head. At this point in the trek, it was all about survival. I followed every command the guide gave, simply saying "here?" as I put my foot on each boulder he told me to step on. I just kept saying "here, here?" as I kept stepping on one boulder after another. He said "yes" as I repeated "here?" I'd touch another boulder and ask "here?" and he'd say "yes." "Here?" "Yes," and so we trekked on.

There is nothing that keeps you moving more than knowing that if you stop, you'll likely die. Then I thought of my mother again. At one point while we were scaling rocks on the side of cliff, I paused to asked, incredulously, while pointing upward, "Are we going up there?" Dastan looked at me as if to say, "Where else are we going?" I thought, *I guess that was a dumb question, considering we are 18,000 feet on the side of a cliff. We certainly can't go down.* So I kept moving.

Finally, we had traversed the area of large rocks known as the "death zone." I was thankful. When we arrived at the crater around 5:00 p.m., I looked at the ice on the crater's rim and pressed my feet into the snow. By this time, my head felt practically disconnected from my body, my legs were aching, my knees scarred from scaling rock cliffs, and I was trying to fight the urge to vomit. I fell to my knees and shouted, "I can't believe it! I can't believe I'm here!" I was now on the crater rim of Mount Kilimanjaro, and the camp was just ahead of me. I fought back tears, looked upward, thanked the Creator, and kept wading through the knee-high glacial snow. A few minutes later, the assistant guide and I arrived at the camp. We were the last to arrive. When we were sighted by my trekking partners, we heard them clapping wildly and yelling, "Yeah! You made it!" To be honest, it was a bit embarrassing, considering that they had been at the camp for at least forty-five minutes. The camaraderie, however, made me feel really good. When I finally made it to my tent, which the porters had already put up, I was completely worn out. My headache alternated between a constant throb and piercing pain.

I was then summoned to dinner. At dinner, I looked at the food and could take only a few bites of the bread and a couple of small spoonfuls of the soup. Afterward, I informed my climbing party that I needed to retire. It took all the energy I could muster just to look at the food, much less eat it. As I got up to leave the table, my hands were shaking, my knees aching. I looked over at the assistant guide, Dastan, who was sitting on the floor under the tent with his fellow porters, smiling as if they had just come back from a relaxing walk in the park. He glanced at me with a smile that seemed to say, "Are you okay? We made it!" I tried to smile, managing to show my teeth. It was more like a grimace. Then I placed my tea on the table and left the communal tent for my toasty sleeping bag. As I turned to leave the tent, I told Nickson that I would not go on to the summit if my head continued to hurt as badly as it was. I did not want to risk having my AMS turn into full-blown HAPE or HACE, I said. I had to be in control of the situation, I told myself. Only I would determine whether I'd go on fighting for the summit. I quickly realized that these thoughts were nothing more than a conversation that I was having with myself, trying to persuade my body that I was in control. It was clear that I was not. After all, who was I fooling? I had long passed the point of no return—the point on the Lemosho route where it is just as dangerous, if not more so, to turn back as it is to continue forward.

Later that evening, in my tent, I rummaged through my medicine bag and began to take anything that remotely applied to my symptoms. I took two ibuprofen tablets given to me by Nickson, who said that ibuprofen was really good for muscle aches. I doubled up on my Diamox tablets, taking two rather than one. An hour or so later, I drank two spoonfuls of Pepto-Bismol for my upset stomach and popped two Tylenol tablets for my excruciating headache. Once I was totally drugged I attempted to fall asleep, but I could not. Every breath felt more like a gasp. I tossed and turned and gasped. It seemed that I was breathing far too rapidly for the small amount of air I was taking into my lungs. Then my thoughts began to wander: Did I let Mom, who was struggling to breathe during the final hours of her life, determine whether to continue fighting for the top?

I then prayed and continued to toss and turn until the next morning, when I awoke before the porters.

Day 7

August 2, 2008

I woke up at 5:00 a.m. to begin preparations for the hike to the summit. When I slipped out of my sleeping bag, it was extremely cold. I am not sure of the temperature, but whatever it was, it was definitely below 0 Fahrenheit. I was colder than I can ever remember being in my entire life! At about 6:00 a.m., I heard a "knock" on the tent, and the words "Morning tea."

"Thanks" I said, as I reached outside the tent to retrieve the tea that the porter had left for me. Then I quickly zipped the tent shut to block out the cold air. Shortly after getting the porter's wakeup call and taking a sip of tea, I began piling on clothes. I put on more clothes than I thought possible: a cotton t-shirt, a long-sleeve wool shirt, a wool turtleneck, two fleece jackets, and a down vest underneath an all-over waterproof down suit and two wool hats. Once I had layered on all these clothes, I emerged from my tent to discover a big problem: I could not move! I went back inside and took off a few layers and reemerged, this time feeling that I was comfortable, even if a bit chilly.

I strapped my headlamp on to my head so that I could make my way to the breakfast tent. I did not eat. I drank one cup of black coffee, then left the tent to assemble with my expedition to begin our pre-dawn trek to the summit. I felt morbidly tired. Ten minutes into the hike, I began shedding clothes and giving them to Dastan as we began to trek uphill. While walking, I silently repeated to myself, "You will not get ill. Go slowly. You can do this." At first I was slow to get going and felt that my own weight was far too much to carry, but I kept going, one foot in front of the other, all the while telling myself: breathe, breathe.

Then I noticed that the team had stopped. The twenty-something woman in front of me was vomiting violently. She fell to her knees, her face pale and blue, repeatedly heaving and vomiting. Nickson alternated between cradling the young woman in his arms and standing behind her to support her as she vomited. Her mom stood by looking sheepishly helpless. I thought to myself how strong she had looked as we were coming up the mountain, and how quickly things change.

I kept moving. By this time, I'd gotten into a rhythm. The sun had come up, and I was at the head of the trekking team. In a strange way, I felt exuberant, vindicated. I remembered the biblical quote: "The first shall become last and the last shall become first." For the first time, I really felt that I was going to make it to the top. As I hiked onward, I saw people gathered together in the glacier snow. I then noticed that they were gathered around a sign that I had seen in pictures many times as I imagined myself atop Mount Kilimanjaro. This sign still seemed very far away, even though it was only a few yards.

Our expedition kept trekking. We were now in a straight line, all looking bedraggled as we trudged through the knee-high snow. When I mustered enough strength to look upward, I declared to the expedition, "I can see victory on the horizon." Sure enough, about ten minutes later, after trudging through the snow and ice, I had reached Kibo, the summit of Mount Kilimanjaro, the roof of Africa! I fell to my knees and kissed Kibo before peering down over the clouds in sheer awe. I was peering down from the highest point in Africa—19,340 feet above sea level. It was unbelievable, a mystical sight. I was amazed at how white everything looked, how surreal and dream-like it was to be up so high, above the clouds on a blanket of snow in a continent known for its warmth. I was spellbound, not quite sure what to think or believe.

I posed with the rest of the expedition to take pictures and shoot video before being hurried down the mountain by Nickson. He was adamant that we not stay at altitude too long, especially given the young woman's fragile condition, so we began our solemn trek down the mountain. On the way down I passed a woman who appeared to be about seventy years of age. She was lying flat on her back and appeared not to be breathing. Her husband was crouched over her perspiring and trying to arouse her as he asked questions of the guide. I could tell he was deeply concerned. I walked past the woman, peering down at her as if viewing a body in a casket. By this time, I had grown accustomed to seeing people in various stages of infirmity, so I did as I had done for the past seven days—I kept moving.

Fig. 2.10. Me standing near the crater rim of Mount Kilimanjaro.

Fig. 2.11 Me at the summit of Mount Kilimanjaro.

Fig. 2.12. Me and Dastan in front of the Uhuru Peak sign at the summit of Mount Kilimanjaro.

Fig. 2.13. Expedition on the summit, from left to right, me, Nickson, Karen, Mori, and Dastan.

Day 8, Final Day

August 3, 2008

At 6:40 a.m., I awakened to loud singing. The porters were singing an Africa chant song called "Ole Kilimanjaro." It was very melodious, reminding me of an old African American spiritual. How nice to hear the harmonic, spiritual singing amidst the rain falling on the leaves in the forest. The porters and guides seem anxious to get going. They are rushing me. I hear them calling, "Daughter! Daughter! Breakfast!" As I heed their command, I have mixed emotions. This will be my last breakfast on the mountain. I feel a tinge of sadness. I am saying good-bye to the mountain, goodbye to a dream.

I quickly snap out of my reverie to a camp that is already abuzz with porters readying breakfast. I try to journal, but the porters seem far more anxious to get going and break camp. I'm sure they are looking forward to bringing this eight-day trek to a close. So I put down my pen and hurriedly place my clothes and other belongings in my rucksack. I go to the communal breakfast tent, but I don't really have time to eat, so I eat two very small slices of watermelon. We then set out with the trekking crew: Nickson, the guide, in the front; Karen, second; her daughter, third; me, forth; and the assistant guide bringing up the rear. I'm sure he probably stayed behind assuming he'd need to walk more slowly with me. As it turns out, that was exactly the case. I tried very hard during this last leg of the trek—indeed the final day—to keep up with the rest of the crew, but my legs simply would not cooperate. There was no way I could do it. I simply could not move at the same speed as the others. I kept leaping (and mostly stumbling) over all the roots and rocks. My legs were killing me. My knees felt like mush. It took all the energy that I could muster to keep placing one foot in front of the other. It seemed as if other people were moving at a much faster clip. One woman, who looked to be about sixty years old, was even ahead of me. I couldn't believe it! The moment I saw her I thought, *I must be in really bad shape!* This thought quickly vanished when, moments later, I saw her being loaded into an emergency rescue van and driven down the mountain. *The race goes not to the swift, but to those who endure,* I thought as I looked at the back of the SUV whisk her away. Later I saw another woman being carried down in a Range Rover jeep. Apparently, she too was unable to descend any further.

As I ambled down the mountain, slipping and stumbling over rocks and tree roots, I came alongside yet another woman who looked absolutely pitiful. Her entire cadence screamed, "I'm in pain!" She and I, ironically, had the same backpack. Just to make small conversation—and to identify with her in some way, as we were both obviously in pain—I asked her where she was from.

"West Virginia," she replied.

I smiled and said, "Oh, I'm from Georgia."

It was obvious that she was barely able to speak. Not wanting her to feel obligated to do so, I kept moving, staying slightly ahead of her. I think she was the only person that I passed and stayed ahead of during my descent. Later she eventually gave up and took a jeep to the foothill. I, on the other hand—my face blackened from the volcanic ash and burned from the sunlight reflecting off the glacier, and my knees scraped and bleeding from scaling the side of the mountain—kept moving. The assistant guide, having determined that I could see the end and that I would be okay, broke rank and headed towards the bus that was waiting to take us to the town of Moshi. Now I was walking alone.

I finally reached the bottom of the mountain—alone. I must admit that at that point, I wanted a celebration. I wanted a big "Kudos! You've done it!" celebration. Instead, there were a bunch of hot sweaty porters, the guide, the assistant guide, a van driver, and the two experienced hikers waiting on the bus with a look on their faces that read, "Come on. Where have you been?"

I was a bit taken aback. Part of me said, "What's the big deal. I paid $3,000USD to climb this mountain! I can take as long as I want," and yet at that very moment, I felt this surge of unimaginable joy and personal achievement. This was the biggest test of endurance and fortitude that I had ever experienced, and I passed it—not with flying colors, but I had passed. I accomplished something that I knew in my heart could be achieved, although I never thought that I would actually achieve it. This was truly one—if not *the only*—moment in my life that would last for an eternity. These moments do not come easily. These are hard-won moments. They show us that we are only human and that God is indeed real! I realized that, although I was sore all over, I was savoring victory with a vengeance. With this sense of personal empowerment, I hopped on to the bus for the ride back to Moshi. While on the bus, I silently reflected on my journey. Africa being my ancestral home, I felt obliged to follow the African tradition of never returning home without a gift. I felt that I had given my spirit to the mountain, now I wanted to give something tangible to the people who were so central to my journey. These people were the porters, guides and the cook. I gave my baklava to one porter, my all-over face cap to another porter, my sleeping pad to the cook, and I left my headlight, the item that was most valuable to me on the trip, with the assistant guide. Later in the day, we arrived in the little town of Moshi, where we had a wonderful meal at a beautiful outdoor restaurant. Before eating, we all gave a toast to our efforts and success. I had fresh fried fish, potatoes, and a soft drink.

After eating, we distributed tips to everyone in our party. The porters appeared extremely satisfied with their tips. Later we boarded the bus again and headed to the Impala Hotel. This was quite different from the rustic and spacious suite at the Ngurdoto Lodge, but it was quite nice as well. We all stood in line in the hotel lobby to have our certificates of accomplishment given to us. Nickson signed each certificate as we waited in line like high school students, waiting to take hold of our diplomas, all beaming with pride. Much like high school graduation, this signaled a new vista in our lives. Later, I said goodnight to my trekking partners, made two telephone calls: one to my sister and the other to my boyfriend, then bought a cup of hot tea from the restaurant/lounge, and retired to my room.

Fig. 2.14. Me at the base of Mount Kilimanjaro after descending 19,340 feet. My boots and gaiters are covered in mud because the rainfall earlier in the day made the trail muddy and soggy.

Day 9, Morning after the Trek

August 4, 2009

The next morning I awoke at about 7:00 a.m. I rolled over in bed, barely able to move. I realized that I had woefully underestimated the assault that the climb would mount against my body. As I rolled over, I reached toward the nightstand and picked up the remote control for the television. I began watching the morning news. A newsflash scrolled across the screen along with the news anchor's announcement: "Three climbers perish on Mount McKinley."

Knowing that the trekking party was supposed to meet in the hotel lobby at 8:00 a.m. to leave for safari at Ngorongoro Park, I picked up the phone and dialed Nickson.

"Good morning, Sheree. We'll see you downstairs shortly?"

"I have a change of plans. I will not be going on safari at the Ngorongoro National Park. I am going to the coast."

He seemed shocked. "Are you sure?"

"Yes," I said. I was thinking, *I need warmth. I need the ocean.*

"Okay," he replied. I hung up the phone and walked over to the short dresser where I had placed my Kilimanjaro certificate the night before. I picked up the certificate and looked at it closely, beaming with pride until I realized that I had not signed it. All of a sudden, I felt an extreme urge to sign the certificate. Frantically, I looked through my muddy duffle bag for an ink pen. There was none. I looked in the night stand drawer. Nothing. Finally, I found a pen under the sheets, and I quickly signed the certificate, as if my life depended on it. It was weird. Afterward, I called to make my flight reservations with Air Tanzania. At around 1:00 p.m., I was on my way to the Island of Zanzibar, where I would spend the next five days sashaying around the island, eating freshly caught fish, and relaxing near the Indian Ocean. It was just what the doctor ordered.

Fig. 2.15. Colobus monkey, indigenous to the Kilimanjaro and Zanzibar regions.

Fig. 2.16. Me on Zanzibar Island the second day after the trek.

CHAPTER 3: WHY TREK MOUNT KILIMANJARO?

There are many reasons people choose to put their bodies through one of the most grueling experiences of their lives Some do it for personal reasons, some do it for spiritual reasons, and others are simply adventurous. Whatever the reason and regardless of one's intentions at the start, in the end, all trekkers will have at least one thing in common, and that is an experience that will be indelibly etched in their minds. They will become members of a small, self-selected group of people on the planet who have touched the snow-capped roof of Africa. Further, if glaciologists are correct in their predictions that by 2020 global warming will have totally removed the snow from Kilimanjaro, then within ten years from the publication of this book, no living creature will ever have the opportunity to touch the *snow-capped* summit of Mount Kilimanjaro again. It is an achievement well worth aspiring toward and savoring!

Trekking Alone

The decision whether to trek with a spouse, partner, or friend is a personal one. For me, the decision was clear. I needed to make the trek alone. First, it was a pragmatic decision. That is, my boyfriend was prone to severe altitude sickness and decided that he was not up to accompanying me to the summit of one of the highest peaks in the world. Second, I knew that it was unlikely that I would find others in my immediate circle of friends who had either the same adventurous spirit or the desire. Third, I felt that I needed to be alone on this trek at this point in my life. To say that you are trekking alone, however, is somewhat of a misnomer, because you are never really alone on the mountain. There are always fellow trekkers, especially if you trek during one of the peak seasons such, as July through August or January through March.

Trekking Alone as a Woman

Some women choose to trek solo without anyone other than their guide and porters. Other women sign up for a trek and later join with a group that they have been placed in by an outfitter. These women usually join larger groups of fifteen to twenty people, and then develop a sense of camaraderie with a smaller team of women within the larger group. While trekking, I saw quite a few middle-aged women who were with groups. You may choose to do as I did and request to be grouped with trekkers with whom you are likely to feel comfortable. In my case, I requested to climb with a small team of women. Honoring my request, the trekking agency put me with a mother-daughter team from the United States (Colorado). Altogether, there were three women trekkers in my expedition, ranging in age from nineteen to mid-fifties. Most of the trekkers I saw on the mountain were couples who appeared to be either German or American. My group of three women was the only all-women's group that I saw during our eight-day trek on the mountain.

If I was going to be part of a group, it was important to me that it be a small one. I really wanted this to be a solo experience as much as possible, and, as it turns out, the group of three women was the perfect size and constitution. It allowed me to be alone, yet have company when I needed to talk with others, either to joke around or to commiserate about the long journey. Also, traveling with a small group allowed me to get more attention from the trekking guides, who kept a close eye on me during the most strenuous parts of the trek. In fact, when I suffered from severe acute mountain sickness (AMS) at an altitude of about 17,000 feet, one guide stayed behind with me in order to trek at a slower pace. It was during this time that I realized the importance of being with a very small team. If you choose to trek with a team, I would strongly advise you to choose a small group, not more than five trekkers. This allows you to receive more individualized attention, and you are under less pressure to keep up with fellow trekkers than you might be in a larger group.

Trekking Alone as an African American Woman

Trekking Kilimanjaro alone is one thing. Trekking alone as a woman is another, and trekking alone as an African American woman is another altogether. I was the only African American woman on the mountain. I saw no African American men. Being the only African American woman trekking on the mountain was an interesting experience. My appearance elicited both interest and curiosity from fellow mountain climbers and guides alike. Most European and American trekkers saw me as a bit of an oddity. Some thought that I was from Moshi or Arusha and part of the Wachagga ethnic group. I suspect that they thought I was a female porter. Others seemed to know that I was American and did not know what to make of me.

Why would a woman of African descent be such an oddity trekking the slopes of Mount Kilimanjaro? The main reason is that most Tanzanians do not aspire to climb to the top of Mount Kilimanjaro, and even if they do, they do not do so because most simply can't afford the clothing and other essentials necessary to make the journey. Therefore, many Europeans have a sense of disbelief that Africans or African Americans can afford such an expensive endeavor. Indeed, it is expensive even for the average American, let alone an African American of modest means, like me. In fact, one night when I returned to the communal eating tent (the mess hall as the porters called it), one of my fellow trekkers from Colorado shared with me that Nickson, our guide, had told her that he has rarely seen African Americans make the trek. Most of them do not have the money to make the journey from America to Africa, and many can't afford the hiking gear, he told her. In all of the fifteen years he had been guiding treks, he had guided only a handful of African Americans. Ironically, one of those African American men, Davine Green, wrote a book that inspired me to take the trek. I sent an email to Mr. Green before leaving for Tanzania. I never received a response.

Many Wachagga women who are fit enough to take the trek and have the resources simply see no sense in making the climb. Many Wachaggas view the mountain in the same way as many of their ancestors did—not as a force of nature to conquer but as a part of nature in which they must live in harmony. It is no surprise, then, that I received quizzical looks from the Wachagga porters, who wondered why a Wachaggan woman would be trekking on Mount Kilimanjaro. I was often greeted by porters, who would say, *"Habari gani"* ("What's the news?" literally, in Swahili. Figuratively, the interpretation is "How are you?") I would respond, *"Asante sana"* ("Very good. Thank you.") Unlike when they greeted Europeans, rather than continue on their way after giving the traditional greeting, they would go on to speak to me using other Swahili phrases, such as *"Uko hapa kwa likizo?"* ("Are you on holiday?") I would either look at them in a puzzled way or respond in broken Swahili with a distinct American accent. Then they would say, or, more often, whisper, *"Nyeusi kimarekani"* (black American). Then our eyes usually met each others with an affectionate gaze, followed by the international language of friendship—a smile—and I would keep trekking.

CHAPTER 4:   LEMOSHO ROUTE

The following are the six established routes, in order of number of days it takes to reach the summit: *Marangu* (5–6 days), *Rongai* (5-6 days), *Umbwe* (5–6 days), *Shira Plateau* (5–8 days), *Machame* (6–7 days), and *Lemosho* (8–10 days).[4] Most people take the Marangu Route to the summit of Mount Kilimanjaro. This route is variously known as the "tourist," "whiskey," and "Coca-Cola" route. The Marangu route is the favorite of tourists and non-hikers because it is one of the shortest and has the lowest incline. It is also the cheapest route, because you summit in four to five days, thus minimizing trekking time and your time on the mountain. Fewer days on the mountain translates into lower costs. The Marangu Route has covered huts that include sleeping carts, and at each rest station along the route, there is an opportunity to purchase cold drinks, including beer and Coca-Cola. That is why it is often referred to as the "Coca-Cola" or "whiskey" route. Most written accounts of trekking Mount Kilimanjaro are based on the Marangu route, because it is the route most traveled.

There are few accounts of people who have trekked the Lemosho route. In fact, in my research, I was not able to locate a single personal account of a trekker who had trekked this path. Compared to other routes, the Lemosho route is far less traveled, longer, more scenic and more strenuous. Trekking to the summit via the Lemosho route takes from eight to ten days, through four different climate zones. You start off in the rainforest, where you will see colobus monkeys, bearded

---

4 Wikipedia, "Mount Kilimanjaro Climbing Routes," http://en.wikipedia.org/wiki/Mount_Kilimanjaro_climbing_routes.

lichen, and white-necked ravens. Later, you'll walk through heath and moorland, where you'll likely spot packs of jackal. Then you'll trek through the alpine desert before ending up on the snow-covered crater, just below the huge glaciers. It really is akin to trekking from the South to the North Pole in eight days to ten days!

The Lemosho Route was pioneered by an American expedition in 2002. It is the only route that ascends from the western part of the mountain. It is longer than other routes, and there is a portion of the route (the Western Breach) that is very steep, with a mean gradient of 26 degrees (Stedman 2006). The Lemosho trail has perhaps the most negative reputation among American trekkers, in part because of a 2006 rockslide near Arrow Glacier Camp that killed four Americans. Due to the melting ice and glaciers, rocks that were previously bound to the mountain became dislodged. While crossing a stretch of the trail for about thirty minutes, the American climbers were hit by a 39-ton glacier deposit, falling some 150 meters and traveling at a speed of 39 meters per second. Afterward, this part of the Western Breach was coined the "death zone" because of the vulnerability of trekkers to falling rock (Stedman 2006).

Sometime later that year, a reconnaissance party was formed to explore the western side of Mount Kilimanjaro with a special emphasis on the Western Breach and the "death zone." The researchers, consisting of a team of glaciologists, geologists, seismologists, and meteorologists, made three recommendations. One called for a route change to divert walkers away from the dangerous section. That way, trekkers would only be in the "death zone" for about five minutes rather than roughly thirty minutes. The second recommendation was to erect a sign at Arrow Glacier to inform trekkers of the risks and dangers of climbing during the day, when the sun is high up in the sky, making it more likely that rockfalls will occur. The third recommendation was to have regular inspections by scientists to assess chances of further rockfall.

After the tragedy, the Western Breach route was closed, and apparently, had only reopened just a few months before I took the trek in 2008. Initially I was apprehensive about the Western Breach and crossing the "death zone." My apprehension notwithstanding, I decided that it was a risk that I was willing to take. This route also requires major rock scrambling. Although this accounts for only about an hour of the entire trek, if you are not accustomed to rock climbing, you may find this to be a bit nerve wracking, as I did. Although the risks are higher compared to those you assume on other routes, so are the gains.

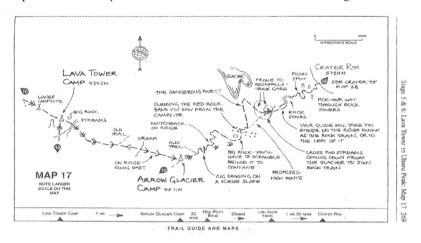

Fig. 4.1. The Western Breach. Note the area just below the glacier where there is falling rock.

Think carefully about the route you choose. You should give consideration to your preference for enjoying the flora and fauna, thoughts about how well you may acclimatize, your level of physical fitness, and whether you'd prefer a more solitary trek or a trek that is a bit more congested. After careful consideration, I decided that I wanted to take a scenic route that would give me the time to fully appreciate the various flora and fauna on the mountain. Although I was confident in my fitness level, I was not sure how I would respond at altitude, so I wanted to take a longer route to provide me with more time to acclimatize. The fact that the route was sparsely traveled was also important, because I was interested in a more peaceful commune with nature. For all of these reasons, I chose the Lemosho Route (also known as the Western Breach Route).

From a trekking standpoint, the major advantage of this route is that it allows you to ascend right on to the crater. This gives the climber the opportunity to inspect the crater and get a close-up view of the glaciers. You spend the night on the crater's rim and summit directly from the crater the following day. Another advantage of the Western

Breach Route is that you summit Mount Kilimanjaro during the day rather than at night. Therefore, you are able to see the gorgeous vistas and the remarkable surroundings. I must admit, though, that if you are prone to vertigo, the occasional vertiginous drops may be problematic. However, when you arrive on the summit from this angle, you will see, as I did, that the risks are well worth the benefits. I highly recommend this route for those who are a bit more adventurous. It is absolutely phenomenal! I simply cannot express just how phenomenal it really is! You'll just have to experience it yourself.

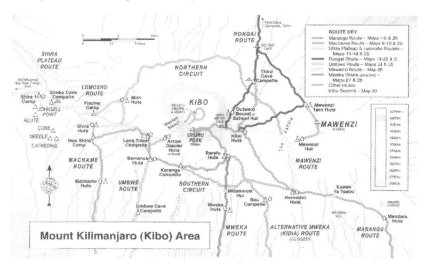

Fig. 4.2. Lemosho Route, reprinted from Stedman 2009.

CHAPTER 5: TREKKING COMPANIES: CHOOSING WHO WILL FACILITATE YOUR TRAVEL

Mount Kilimanjaro is a national park, and according to national authorities, you are not permitted to trek Mount Kilimanjaro without a guide. It is not necessary to sign up with a trekking company in order to get a guide, however. You can simply show up at one of the local trekking companies in Tanzania—most likely Arusha—and hire a guide and as many porters as you'd like. Choosing your own guide is cheaper, but it is not necessarily safe. Thus, most people hire a trekking company to facilitate their trek.

While in the United States, I conducted quite a bit of research before deciding on the trekking company that I would use. I found literally hundreds of companies offering service on Mount Kilimanjaro. After a considerable amount of time searching the Internet, I narrowed my search down to three companies: Alpine Ascents International[5], Kilisummit Adventures and Safari[6], and Ultimate Kilimanjaro[7]. Ultimately, I decided to go with Kilisummit Adventures and Safari. Table 1 below shows the 2008 costs of the three companies and the

---

5   Alpine Ascents International, "Mount Kilimajaro" http://www.alpineascents.com/kilimanjaro.

6   Kilisummit Adventure & Safari LLC, "Kilisummit, Mt. Kilimanjaro" http://kilisummit.com/kilisummit_home.

7   Ultimate Kilimanjaro: Your Kilimanjaro Specialist, "Climb Mount Kilimanjaro" http://www.ultimatekilimanjaro.com.

major considerations that lead to my decision about whether to hire the trekking company.

Table 1. Comparison of Trekking Companies

Trekking company	Cost	Considerations/deciding factors
Alpine Ascents	$5,700	• Cost exorbitant; offered several unnecessary features (e.g., portable oxygen, communications, and cybercasts) • No local guide
Kilisummit Adventure and Safari	$3,183	• Company used local guides • United States liaison (There was a person I could speak with comfortably and personally in the USA) • Provided "custom" small groups with little additional cost • Well known local guide who is the owner and operator (offered an opportunity to support local business)
Ultimate Kilimanjaro	$1,685	• Difficulty contacting someone directly • Small group not available; traveling with a guide alone required additional planning and resources

My list of trekking companies is obviously not exhaustive. It shows the top three trekking companies that emerged from my research, based on *my* needs. My hope is that it will give you some idea about my considerations, and why I chose one over the other. None of these companies may meet your needs. You may find other companies that are far more suitable than those that I have listed here. Further, you may have different criteria that you are considering in your choice. Whatever the situation, as the old saying goes, you must be careful about the company you keep. The correct trekking outfitter can literally mean the difference between life and death.

When deciding on a company, a major consideration for me was that I would be traveling alone. I wanted to be sure that I had enough structure in the planning so that I would not have to worry about anything major from the time I landed at the Kilimanjaro airport up to the point when I descended the mountain. I also decided that I'd prefer an American operator, because of the ease of communication and their familiarity with American standards and customs. Beyond that, I searched for companies that employed local guides. To me, it was important that the guide be someone who knew the local culture and customs. After contacting several companies, I found that the cost varied from approximately $1,600 USD for the cheapest trek to nearly $6,000 USD for the most expensive trek (both totals excluding airfare). Kilisummit's pricetag was somewhere in the middle, and the total cost of my trek was $3,100 USD (excluding airfare). Kilisummit was an outstanding outfitter. One of the many things I found appealing about Kilisummit is that the company is still fairly small, so there is a personal flair to their service. For instance, when I had questions about the itinerary, I was offered a telephone number that I could call and talk with the proprietor personally. During the conversation, I could ask any questions that emerged during the conversation, rather than send a typed list of the questions over the Internet. Natalie, the proprietor in America, was very personable and followed up with me to share details and to see if I had other questions or concerns. I found this personal attention particularly comforting, because it helped to know that there was a real person backing many of the claims that are made on the Web site. As we talked over the phone, Natalie informed me that my guide would be a young man by the name of Nickson. I had already read about Nickson in my previous research. His work as a guide was highly touted. I was also informed that Natalie would be in Kilimanjaro on the day of the trek and that it would be possible for us to meet face to face. This was also reassuring.

Kilisummit is basically an agent for the local company Masai Giraffe. Masai Giraffe is a local trekking company staffed and managed by local Wachagga people. Nickson Moshi, the company's owner and operator, is Wachagga and has a long history of guiding and trekking Mountain Kilimanjaro.

Nickson worked his way to the top. As a little boy, he would stand near the beginning of the trail and watch the *msungas* (white people) select men and boys to work as porters for the wealthy, white, mainly male trekkers. At that time, Nickson told me that he was a scrawny little boy and much too lightweight to work as a porter. He was also still in primary school. Once he completed primary school, he sought a job as a porter. At this time, he was tall and as strong as his male counterparts. He was eventually selected for the position of porter. After working several years as a porter, Mr. Moshi took the certification test to become a guide. Becoming a guide requires a fair amount of resources, as one has to pay to take the certification course. After working as a guide for many trekking operators, Nickson ventured out on his own and began leading groups through his private trekking company.

The services offered by Masai Giraffe were superb. Nickson is so observant with respect to what is happening with the group. At one point along the trek, he noticed that I was falling behind the others. I was not aware that I was getting slower and slower, although I was feeling a bit tired. It was at this point that Nickson instructed the assistant guide to "stay behind" with me and walk at a much slower pace, while Nickson proceeded at a faster pace with the other women in our group. As it turned out, this was absolutely the best decision, because I did not realize how tired I truly was until we arrived at the next campsite later that evening and I was barely able to stand. Nickson and the assistant guide, Dastan, showed this level of attentiveness throughout the trip.

Chapter 6:   How Should You
Prepare for Your Kilimanjaro Trek?

Ideally, you should begin preparing to climb Mount Kilimanjaro well in advance of your actual travel date, at least 90 to 120 days prior to leaving the country. I began intense trip preparation about 90 days from the time I booked my flight.

Finances

The one thing that is consistent from everything I've read—and you'll ever read—is that a major factor to take into consideration is money. Unless you have a major inheritance, an endless supply of cash, or $8,000 to $10,000 grand lying around to burn, you will need to save plenty of money for your Kilimanjaro adventure. By far the largest expense for the trip was my airline ticket and trekking company costs. Of course, there are those who solicit corporate or charity group sponsors, and then there are the rest of us, who must scrimp and save. Once I had my money in order and had purchased my airline ticket, I was able to plan the logistics of my trip. (See appendix A for an itemization of trip costs.)

Timing

According to the Kilimanjaro climbing calendar, the best times to climb Kilimanjaro are between late June and August or between January and March. Other times of the year are considered the rainy season, and according to trekking agencies they are to be avoided. I traveled in late July and the weather was great for trekking. It was cool and dry in the afternoon, and warm and sunny during the day. It was drizzling rain on the very last day of the trek. After having trekked through slogs of mud on the way down the mountain on the last day, I can only imagine what it must be like to trek during the rainy the season. The terrain, in large part, will determine how easy it will be for you to summit Kilimanjaro.

Travel Arrangements

When planning your travel, take note of the airlines with flights to Kilimanjaro Airport during the season that you will be traveling. At the time of this publication, there are only three international airlines with flights from the United States to Kilimanjaro, Tanzania. They are Ethiopian Airlines, Air France, and Lufthansa. I began monitoring flights leaving the United States for Kilimanjaro, Tanzania, about six months prior to leaving. Typically, I plan vacation trips two to three months in advance. Planning for this trip was different. I started planning about six months in advance, and it required quite a bit of organization. I had to juggle lots of things, such as requesting time off from work, scheduling doctors' appointments and clinic visits, making time for physical training, calling and emailing trekking companies, making long-term daycare arrangements for my dog, and finally making flight arrangements.

Using the Internet, I was able to compare ticket costs for all the airlines flying to Kilimanjaro. Therefore, it was not necessary for me to make flight arrangements with a travel agency. I went online once or twice a week to look at available flights to Kilimanjaro, Tanzania. I began looking earlier in the year, around January 2008. During the months of January through May, I continued to watch the cost of flights to see whether fares were increasing or decreasing. With the price of fuel rising, it was clear that I should book my flight by April if I wanted to take advantage of the ninety-day booking promotion as well as lock in a ticket price before the cost of gasoline skyrocketed any further. I chose an itinerary that would allow me to stop in route and change planes, allowing me to deplane and get some fresh air before continuing my journey. I am extremely uncomfortable on long flights that do not allow me to get off and stretch and breathe fresh air.

I confirmed and booked my flight about two months in advance of leaving. I booked a domestic flight on United Airlines and an international flight on Ethiopian Airlines. I left Atlanta, Georgia, on July 20, 2008, at 5:40 a.m. and arrived in Washington, D.C., at 7:23 a.m. I departed Washington, D.C., at 10:05 a.m. on Ethiopian Airlines and flew to Rome, Italy. I arrived in Rome at 12:40 a.m. on July 21. I did not change planes in Italy. From Rome, I flew to Addis Ababa, Ethiopia, arriving at 8:20 a.m. I had a two-hour layover, which allowed me to stretch, walk around, and breathe a bit of fresh air. In Ethiopia, I boarded another Ethiopian Airlines plane and headed to Nairobi, Kenya. I stayed on the airplane when we stopped in Kenya at 12:00 p.m. and left at 12:45 p.m. Afterward, I flew on to Kilimanjaro, Tanzania. I arrived in Kilimanjaro, Tanzania, at 1:45 p.m. on Monday, July 21. By this time, I had been en route for about twenty-three hours. However, when I arrived I was more excited than exhausted. Fortunately, when I arrived at the Kilimanjaro Airport, there was plenty of daylight left. I was able to clear customs, and retrieve my bags without any problems. After retrieving my bags, per instructions from the Kilisummit Trekking Company representative, I awaited my driver, who arrived at the small, non-descript airport holding a sign that read, "Sheree Marshall." The driver delivered me to the Ngurdoto Lodge, in Dodoma, where I would be staying for the next five days preceding my Mount Kilimanjaro trek.

Vaccinations

After getting your physical exam, you'll want to be sure that you have all of your vaccinations necessary to travel to Tanzania[8]. Make sure that your vaccinations are recorded on your vaccination card at the time they are administered. The required vaccines may change over the years depending on whether or not there is a current epidemic of disease. There is no reason to be overly concerned about an epidemic. I have traveled to sub-Saharan Africa enough times to know that epidemics

---

8   Centers for Disease Control and Prevention, "Vaccines and Immunizations" http://www.cdc.gov/vaccines.

in certain countries are no cause for alarm. It simply means that you should be protected through vaccines and behave in ways that do not place you at risk of contracting disease.

First, it is important that you are up to date on all your vaccinations required for the United States. For most adults in the United States, the required vaccinations are tetanus, diphtheria, and pertussis (Td/Tdap), measles, mumps, rubella, varicella, hepatitis A, hepatitis B, and meningococcal. You'll need the meningococcal vaccination only if you have specific risk factors[9]. After receiving the required U.S. immunizations, you can turn your attention to getting vaccinated for your Tanzanian trip. In July 2008, I found that the vaccination recommendations for Tanzania were consistent with those recommended several years earlier. I also updated my tetanus vaccine, and I decided that I'd go ahead and take the meningococcal vaccine, as it is recommended for travel to Tanzania. I was generally up to date on most of my vaccinations. Because I have traveled to Africa frequently over the past ten years, I had already received several of the recommended vaccines prior to my Tanzanian trip.

You should schedule a pre-travel visit with a travel clinic well in advance of the travel date. You can easily locate a travel clinic near you by doing an Internet search. I would highly recommend that you see a physician who is a *high-altitude specialist*, as opposed to a mere travel specialist. Both types of specialists are usually on staff at travel clinics. Visiting a physician who specializes in tropical medicine may be a good idea as well. It is also helpful to consult the Centers for Disease Control and Prevention's (CDC) Web site for overseas travel[10]. As an employee of the CDC, I was able to get expert advice onsite at the employee health clinic. I also had ready access to the Emory travel clinic, a medical facility associated both with the CDC and the Emory University School of Medicine. Because I was not traveling on behalf of the United States government, it was not possible for the CDC clinic to administer all of the vaccinations; however, I was able to consult with a travel nurse and get the final shots in the hepatitis series. Fortunately, that left me with

---

9 Centers for Disease Control and Prevention, "Immunization Schedules" http://www.cdc.gov/vaccines.

10 Centers for Disease Control and Prevention, "Travelers Health" http://www.cdc.gov/travel.

few vaccinations to complete by the time I arrived at the Georgia State Health Department's health clinic for vaccinations.

Most of the vaccinations are more easily administered from a travel clinic or your State Health Department's health clinic rather than your private physician, because many physicians do not routinely stock some of the vaccines you'll need, such as those for yellow fever and rabies. For travel advice and vaccinations, I visited the Emory Travel Clinic in Atlanta, Georgia, and the Georgia State Health Department rather than my private physician. Depending on how often you've traveled in developing countries, you may need several vaccines in preparation for your Tanzania trip.

At the health and travel clinics, the purpose of the vaccinations will be explained to you, and they will likely give you a schedule of the days when you should report back for any vaccines that require multiple doses. I was required to take typhoid and yellow fever. I decided not to get vaccinated against rabies, because the vaccine is in short supply and I reasoned that I would not come into close contact with animals. In hindsight, I wish I had taken the vaccine. The four-striped grass mouse is very common above the tree line on Mount Kilimanjaro, and if I had been bitten by a rabies-infected four-striped grass mouse, it would have been necessary for me to get a helicopter into Nairobi, Kenya, in order to be treated. Although I had purchased a health insurance policy to cover the cost of the evacuation, it was not my desire to leave the mountain in a helicopter. My preference, obviously, was to hike to the bottom. Therefore, I would suggest taking the rabies vaccine, because you simply never know what might happen. Better safe than sorry.

I'd also advise you to be well informed prior to attending the health clinic. During my clinic visit, I found myself validating what I had already read on CDC's and other travel Web sites (e.g., World Health Organization[11] and Travel Medicine[12]) rather than trying to absorb totally new information. Therefore, during my travel clinic appointment, I was able to ask more questions that clarified rather than gave me new information. I felt empowered to ask questions and felt more in control of my travel. As a single woman traveling without a companion, I

---

11 World Health Organization, "International Travel and Health", http://www.who.int.

12 Stuart R. Rose and Jay S. Keystone. Travel Medicine: Products & Information for Safe Travel, "International Travel Health Guide",http://www.travmed.com.

needed to be self-reliant and prepared for as many contingencies as possible. For me, this sense of empowerment was very important.

Table 2. Vaccinations Received in Preparation for the Trek

(Information taken from printed material at CDC, Department of Health and Human Services, Centers for Disease Control and Prevention, National Immunization Program, http://www.cdc.gov/vaccines/pubs/vis/default.htm).

Vaccination	Disease	Immunization schedule
Hepatitis A	Hepatitis A is a serious liver disease caused by the hepatitis virus (HAV). HAV can be found in the stool of people with hepatitis A. It is usually spread by coming in contact with food or drinking water, or personal contact with a person who is infected with Hep A.	The shot should be given at least one month before traveling. If you are scheduled to leave in less than one month you may be able to get a shot called immune globulin (IG). IG gives immediate, temporary protection.
Hepatitis B	Hepatitis B is a serious disease that affects the liver. Hepatitis B virus is spread through contact with blood or other body fluids of an infected person.	This shot is given either in a series of 3 or 4 shots. The series provides long-term protection from Hep B; possibly even a lifetime.
Yellow fever	Yellow fever is a serious disease caused by the yellow fever virus. The virus is spread through the bite of an infected mosquito. Yellow fever cannot be spread from person to person.	You will need to receive only one shot that will provide protection for up to 10 years. If it has been longer than 10 years since you last had a shot for yellow fever, you will need to have a booster shot before traveling to Tanzania.

Typhoid	Typhoid is a serious disease that is caused by bacteria called *Salmonella typhil*. People get typohid fever from drinking contaminated water or food.	One dose provides protection. It should be given 2 weeks before travel to allow the vaccine time to work. The vaccine is good for 2 years; you'll need a booster if you are traveling to an endemic place within two years.
Rabies	Rabies is a serious disease caused by a virus. Mainly animals are infected with rabies, but humans can get rabies if they are bitten by infected animals.	The rabies vaccine should be taken in 3 doses: Dose 1 is given before exposure; dose 2 is given 7 days after dose 1; and dose 3 is given 21 or 28 days after dose 1. Booster doses are not recommended for travelers. You are also able to be vaccinated after exposure provided you are able to get to a doctor immediately to get 5 doses within a specified number of days following being bitten by a rabid animal.

Medication

While on the mountain, you will likely be relying only on yourself for medication and other necessary survival supplies you'll need. Most trekking companies do not provide medical support beyond minimal first-aid. Others offer more advanced support, such as pulse oximeters, but at a premium cost. Therefore, it is best that you educate yourself about the various medications before you leave for your trek. After doing a bit of research on high-altitude illnesses, I visited Emory's travel clinic in Atlanta, Georgia. Before the visit, I was aware of several medicines used to treat high-altitude symptoms: Diamox (Acetazolamide), Decadron (Dexamethasone), Nifedipine, and Furosemide. Diamox has a long track record in the prevention and treatment of Acute Mountain Sickness (AMS). The way Diamox works is that it blocks an enzyme in the kidney and makes the blood more acidic. The brain interprets this acidity as a signal to increase breathing. Thus, Diamox enhances your physiological response to altitude by making you breathe more frequently and more deeply; thereby assisting your acclimatization.[13] When I visited the travel clinic, I requested and was prescribed Diamox. I also requested Decadron, although my online research indicated that the drug makes people feel better by alleviating their symptoms, not by helping them acclimatize. This can be dangerous, because it may lead people to think that it is okay to continue to climb higher, when they are not aware that their physiological state has not improved. Because of the tendency of the drug to mask the symptoms of AMS without any appreciable physiologic improvement, it is recommended that the drug be used only in the event that a person with severe AMS or HACE (High Altitude Cerebral Edema) is being evacuated. When Decadron is taken, the person should not climb any higher until Decadron has been discontinued for at least twenty-four hours. That's why the travel specialist who prescribed Decadron did so with the precaution that I remembered each time I looked at the tiny pill: "If you take this, you should be *descending.*" My doctor would prescribe only two pills. Fortunately, I did not need to take them.

Because of the strict rules enforced by most airlines, I did not carry any medicine in my carry-on bags; rather, I packed them with checked luggage. A potential problem with checking your medication is that if your bags are lost you will be without medication, and this could cause a major problem, particularly if these are drugs required for diagnosed medical conditions. If there is a concern, you may want to get clearance for taking your medication with you on the flight. During the trek, I carried all my medicine in a Ziploc plastic bag that I kept with me at all times. Table 3 shows the prescription drugs that I took with me. I carried all of my meds in the original bottles so that I knew the dosage and, if necessary, could report medications to a healthcare provider.

---

13 CIWEC Clinic: Travel Medicine Center, "Altitude Illness Advice for the Trekker", http://www.ciwec-clinic.com.

Table 3. Prescription Drugs Taken on the Trek

(Note: These are the medications prescribed to me and are not meant to represent all of the medication you will need during your trip. Please consult a physician for medical advice pertaining to your specific health condition.)

Drug	Brand name	Treatment (Reason for taking)
Acetazolamide, 125 mg	Diamox	Used to prevent and reduce symptoms of altitude sickness. It is taken to reduce headache, nausea, dizziness, and shortness of breath that can occur when you climb to high altitudes over 10,000 feet (3,048 meters). I took this medication as a prophylactic. I began taking Diamox 3 days before the trek and, continuously, as prescribed during the trek.
Ciprofloxacin, 500 mg	Cipro	An antibiotic used to treat bacterial infections. I took this along just in case I got a bad case of diarrhea due to a bacterial infection.
Dexamethason, 4 mg	Decadron	A corticosteroid hormone used to decrease symptoms such as swelling and allergic-type reactions. It is used to treat breathing problems. I brought this medication as a backup to take if the Diamox was ineffective in reducing my breathing problems.
Doxycycline, 100 mg	Vibramycin	This is an antibiotic that is used to treat bacterial infections, including those that cause acne. It is also used to prevent malaria.

| Mefloquine, 250 mg | Lariam | This medication is used to treat and prevent malaria. I took Mefloquine regularly with the intention of taking Doxycycline if Mefloquine caused me to experience depression. |
| Metronidazole, 250 mg | Flagyl | This is an antibiotic that is used to treat a variety of infections. It stops the growth of bacteria and protozoa. |

Physical and Mental Fitness

Even in the best weather, your chances of reaching the summit are better if you are in good physical and mental condition. The first order of business, after you establish your travel date, is preparing your body for the physical stamina needed for the trek. Physical preparation should take the form of healthy eating and regular physical fitness. Mental preparation involves taking stock of your motivations for climbing and assessing your mental state.

Physical Fitness

Climbing requires strength and endurance. The single most important factor in maximizing the likelihood that you'll reach the summit is your physical fitness. The first thing you should do is visit your primary physician and seek counsel regarding any chronic conditions that may impact or preclude your climbing the mountain (e.g., hypertension, diabetes, asthma). After getting the okay from your doctor, you are well advised to start a physical fitness training program. Being physically fit will allow your body to perform at peak condition while expending less energy than would be required if you were not physically fit. I must admit that I did not schedule a doctor's visit within ninety days of my trip. However, I was confident that I did not have any medical conditions, because I have annual medical exams and had not been made aware of any medical problems at my last doctor's visit. If you are not already physically active, it is critical that you start a moderate exercise program once you have solidified your travel plans. I recommend that you start a rigorous physical training program at least 90 to 120 days prior to your trip. It is important to choose a fitness program that works for you. Ask yourself whether you work better with a personal trainer or train better alone. You might want to also consider whether it is possible for you to sustain a structured exercise regimen or use a more varied routine.

Like most women, I am very busy. I work a full-time job during the day and teach college courses in the evenings. My weekends are usually packed with to-do lists and several tasks and errands, not to mention that I have to take care of a high-strung dog. Therefore, it was best for me to work my fitness routine into my normal daily activities, rather than schedule structured time at the gym with a personal trainer. Given how full my schedule was during the time I began training, I mainly focused on cardiovascular conditioning and endurance. Owing to my cardiovascular training, perhaps, the ascent was not tough or challenging in regard to muscular or cardiovascular fitness. The descent, on the other hand, was an enormous strain on my upper legs and knee joints. In hindsight, I wish I had done more strength training in preparation for the descent. I chose to integrate my training into my day by adding physical fitness exercises to ordinary daily tasks. For instance, I began to look at ways that I could incorporate physical activity into my daily commute to work. So I rode my bike to and from my office, a ten-mile roundtrip. On some occasions, I detoured and took a longer, more hilly route to my home to get the added benefit of a more strenuous cardio workout. I also looked at ways that I could be active during the weekend while doing things that I normally do, like walking my dog. So I began to walk my dog two or three miles rather than simply around the neighborhood. I also added training days. I started going to the fitness center on Sunday afternoons. I have been running for several years and I continued running about two miles every other day. After teaching class in the evenings, I also spent more time in the fitness center at the university.

While working out at the fitness center, I checked my blood pressure and pulse rate regularly. This was important, because I wanted to have a baseline of my working and resting heart rate. As it turned out, this was very useful when I began suffering from acute mountain sickness and had a resting heart rate of 146! I knew that this was high—considering that I was resting. I worked out a minimum of four times per week. My typical routine at the fitness center was thirty minutes on the treadmill, with the incline set at five and the speed set at five. As the time neared for me to leave for the trek, I increased my time on the treadmill to 45 minutes, increased the speed to 10, and increased the incline to 6 (highest is 7). I walked wherever it was practical to do so. For instance, I took mass transit to social functions because this allowed me to ride my bike and walk to and from the train station. I did not train the week I was scheduled to leave. I did not want to get injured, and I had also read that you should allow your body to rest immediately before leaving for the climb.

In addition to working out daily, I also monitored what I ate for several months before leaving. See my food log for the week of May 7, 2008 in Appendix C. I recorded the types and amounts of food that I ate for 3 months prior to traveling. I kept a food log, because I did not want to put on more pounds before leaving, as it is easier to trek over four to seven miles a day if you are not overweight. Keeping a log helped me to keep my pre-Kilimanjaro weight under control, and it also allowed me to monitor the types of food I was eating to be sure that I was eating healthy. I focused on eating fruits and vegetables and cut down on my portions in order to maintain a caloric intake of 1200 calories per day. By the time I left for Mount Kilimanjaro on July 18, my five-foot, three-inch frame was carrying 118 pounds and I felt that I had done a fairly decent job of preparing myself for the strenuous activity in which I was about to engage.

Mental Fitness

Becoming mentally fit can be a bit harder, in part because there is no one way to become mentally prepared, and the definition of "mentally fit" differs from person to person. The most important aspect of preparing mentally is to think positively. While working out at the fitness center, I wore headphones so that I could listen to inspirational messages about life and perseverance. I also purposely avoided sharing my ambition with people who I knew would try to discourage me. That way, I assured myself that I was not consumed with negative thoughts while I was training.

As someone who has dealt with subclinical depression for many years, I have always "self-medicated" through exercise. Although I did not request antidepressants, I was aware that some anti-malarials heighten feelings of depression. Being aware of this allowed me to be proactive and practice cognitive strategies, such as repeating phrases from the Bible. I was also aware that hiking without a close companion might increase my sense of isolation and trigger depression. In fact, I found that the solitary walking experience on the mountain was very helpful; it was stress relieving and allowed me to fall into an almost hypnotic state. However, the isolation did arouse feelings of sadness during the latter part of the trek. If you are prone to depression, you may want to prepare yourself with medication or behavioral strategies to assist you with managing your depression.

High-Altitude Preparation

High altitude is defined based on the following scale:

- High: 8,000 to 12,000 feet (2,438 to 3,658 meters)
- Very high: 12,000 to 18,000 feet (3,658 to 5,487 meters)
- Extremely high: 18,000 feet (5,500 + meters and above) [14]

Most people have not gone to extremely high altitudes, so it is hard for scientists to predict how individuals will respond at very high altitudes. However, it is known that most people who do not reach the summit of Mount Kilimanjaro most often fail because of altitude sickness rather than poor fitness (Berzuchka 2005).

At sea level, the oxygen concentration is about 21 percent, and the barometric pressure averages 760 mm HG. As you ascend higher, the concentration of the oxygen is the same, but you are breathing in fewer molecules per breath.[15] In order to adjust to the smaller number of molecules, your body increases your breathing rate so that you are

14 Rick Curtis, *Outdoor Action Guide to High Altitude: Acclimatization and Illnesses*, http://www.princeton.edu/~oa/safety/altitude.html.
15 Ibid.

breathing faster even at rest. The extra ventilation increases the oxygen level in the blood, but the level is still lower than what it would be at sea level. At the top of Mount Kilimanjaro, you inhale only 50 percent of the oxygen molecules that you breathe in at sea level (Berzuchka 2005). While breathing in less oxygen per breath, the oxygen required for physical exertion remains the same, so that your body has to perform the same activities with less oxygen.

The major cause of altitude sickness is going too high too fast. When you take longer to climb, you decrease your chances of altitude sickness, perform better, and will have a much more enjoyable time. Provided you give your body enough time, your body can adjust to the higher altitudes. At every altitude to which you ascend, your body adjusts once more. So when you ascend to a height of 10,000, your body adjusts physiologically to an altitude of 10,000. When you move above that altitude, your body readjusts again, and so on. This process of adjusting is called *acclimatization* (Bezruchka 2005). Acclimatization is the process by which your body adapts physiologically to the decrease in oxygen molecules at a specific altitude. During acclimatization, several changes take place in the body:

- the depth of your respiration increases, as does the pressure in your pulmonary arteries;
- your body begins to produce more red blood cells to carry the increased oxygen load; and
- there is an increase in the enzyme called carbonic anhydrase, which speeds up the release of oxygen from the hemoglobin to other tissues in the body.[16]

As your body responds physiologically, you should respond *behaviorally*. One behavior to start is to drink plenty of water. You'll likely perspire more and become dehydrated if you do not drink enough water. Keep in mind that you will urinate more at altitude and that your urine should be copious and clear. Some recommend that you drink four to five liters a day (Carmicheal and Stoddard 2002). Your eating habit on the mountain is important as well. Eating mostly complex carbohydrates (e.g., starches, such as potatoes) and simple carbohydrates

---

16   Ibid.

(fruits) throughout your trek is highly recommended, because these foods breakdown to provide the body with much-needed energy. Dried fruits and nuts and various forms of trail mix turned out to be a fantastic snack for me. I took three huge bags of trail mix. At the end of the trek I had only a quarter of one bag left.

Almost everyone who ascends Mount Kilimanjaro will experience acute mountain sickness (AMS), although the severity may vary. Contrary to what one might think, altitude sickness does not come on suddenly, but appears gradually and progresses (Berzuchka 2005). The fact that AMS is a progressive condition allows you to control and monitor your symptoms. The onset and severity of AMS will depend on your elevation, your rate of ascent, and your susceptibility to altitude sickness. You probably have mild AMS if you are experiencing a combination of the following symptoms: headache, dizziness, shortness of breath, nausea, general malaise, and lack of appetite. Mild AMS does not interfere with normal activity and will subside after two to four days.[17]

As long as the symptoms are such as those described above, you can continue to ascend at a moderate rate. If, in addition to the symptoms associated with those listed for mild AMS, you have a headache that is not relieved by medicine, you begin vomiting, and you experience difficulty walking and standing (i.e., ataxia), along with an altered mental state, you are experiencing a more severe form of AMS and should consider immediate descent. There are two severe forms of AMS: high altitude pulmonary edema (HAPE) and high altitude cerebral edema (HACE). Each results from a leakage of fluid through the capillary walls into either the lungs or the brains. HAPE occurs when fluid leaks out of the capillaries into the lungs. HAPE is expected if, in addition to other milder symptoms of AMS mentioned earlier, you experience extreme shortness of breath and begin to cough. This shortness of breath will be apparent even when you are resting. You will likely experience tightness in the chest, accompanied by extreme fatigue and a feeling of suffocation while you are sleeping at night. The coughing may indicate a fluid buildup in your lungs. The fluid buildup in your lungs prevents oxygen exchange (Berzuchka 2005). As the level of oxygen in the bloodstream decreases, this may lead to

---

17 Ibid.

cyanosis, impaired cerebral function, and death. If HAPE is suspected, you should descend immediately. The second severe form of AMS is high altitude cerebral edema (HACE). HACE occurs when fluid leaks out of the capillary walls into the brain. With HACE, you will experience ataxia (lack of coordination, particularly during walking) in addition to headache, loss of appetite, and extreme fatigue. Again, these are symptoms that occur with mild AMS, as mentioned earlier. It is apparent that there are some symptoms that are similar across all forms of altitude sickness, such as headache.

A major harbinger of altitude illness is the lack of recovery from exhaustion even after dramatically decreasing your pace or after resting. Determining whether you have adequately recovered from exhaustion can be difficult because it is not always clear how to measure recovery given that you will likely continue to experience some level of fatigue. Therefore, you should continue to monitor your body closely, checking your vital signs frequently. For instance, I began taking my pulse rate when we stopped to rest and in the tent at night. I then considered all the symptoms together, checked them against those listed in the pocket guide, and put the schematic in my mind to determine a probable diagnosis. I had determined that I would reconsider continuous assent if I believed that my symptoms warranted more acclimatization or that I began the descent—irrespective of the advice of my trekking guide. This was important, because I decided early on, even before I began to feel ill, that I would not risk death to make it to the summit. I must admit, though, that this is not an easy truce to make with yourself after you have reached a certain point. There is always some part of you that will say, "You can do it. Keep going, no matter what the cost." After all, we are adventure seekers; otherwise, we would not have chosen to make the trek in the first place.

The purpose of mentioning altitude illness here is not to make a thorough diagnosis but to provide key signals that indicate when you are moving from one form of altitude sickness to another, more serious, form. You may find it helpful to read a more thorough guide on altitude illness. I carried a pocket guide entitled *Altitude Illness: Prevention and Treatment* by Stephen Bezruchka (2005, 2nd ed.) in my backpack. I found this pocket guide to be extremely useful, particularly as I was beginning to experience altitude sickness at about 15,000 feet. I referenced the guide frequently in order to make an informed decision about whether it was safe for me to continue my journey up the mountain.

There is no way that you can be certain of how you will perform at altitude. You can be in perfectly good physical condition and still not make it to the top of Mount Kilimanjaro. You can't even be certain that your body will perform the same way at the same altitude at different times. There seems to be no sure way of knowing why some people can summit Mt. Kilimanjaro while others can't make it past Gilman's Point (second lowest point below the summit). Some propose that your adjustment to altitude is genetically controlled. There used to be just three cures for treating altitude sickness: descend, descend, and descend. Today there are other options, but not many. Because people have the option of taking drugs and using more sophisticated equipment (such as the hyperbaric bag) they are more likely to take greater risks, and sometimes these risks can be fatal. The two best ways to prepare for the high altitudes are *acclimatization* and *drug therapy* (Berzuchka 2005).

In an effort to acclimatize, I flew into Kilimanjaro four days earlier than the date my trek was scheduled to begin. This gave my body time to pre-acclimatize to a higher altitude, although lower than the altitude to which I would ascend later in my trip. I found this pre-acclimatization very useful, because I live in the state of Georgia, located at the foothills of the Blue Ridge mountains at an elevation of only 738 to 1,050 feet above sea level. In Tanzania, before the trek, I took day trips to into Arusha, the larger city bordering Kilimanjaro. It was an enjoyable time. I spent time at the Ngurdoto Lodge, relaxing, being catered to by all of the hosts and hostesses, reading, and journaling. All the while, my body was adjusting to functioning at this level, while I was expending energy and breathing at an altitude of approximately 5,000 feet. During this time, I began taking Diamox (Acetazolamide), the prescription drug most recommended for those at altitude. Diamox is the one of only two altitude medications that can be taken prophylactically.. This means that you are able to take the drug *prior to* ascending, to assist your body with acclimatization and to prevent altitude sickness. You can also continue taking Diamox as you ascend higher to treat altitude sickness. Since it takes a while for Diamox to take effect, it is recommended that you begin taking Diamox at least twenty-four hours prior to ascent and continue to take the drug as you are ascending. I actually took the medication (only two pills) while I was still in the United States to be sure that my body would be able to tolerate the drug, as some people are known to have allergic reactions.

There is no universally agreed upon dosage. I took the dosage recommended by the physician (250 mg, each day) two days prior to the beginning of my trek and continued taking Diamox tablets twice daily while trekking. I took 125 mg after breakfast and another 125 mg after dinner. Because Diamox is a diuretic, you will have to urinate often. This means it is important for you to drink plenty of water. Many high-altitude specialists recommend drinking at least four quarts (liters) of fluid each day. Other side effects of the drug are tingling of the hands, blurring of vision, and an altered sense of taste. I did not have blurred vision or an altered sense of taste, but my lips and fingers tingled. I must say that compared to the symptoms of AMS, these were minor inconveniences. I also had a prescription for Decadron (Dexamethasone), a steroid that decreases brain swelling and reverses the effects of AMS. Another prescription in which you may be interested is Nifedipine, a calcium blocker that lowers pressure in the pulmonary artery[18]. Although Nifedipine has been shown to prevent HAPE in experimental studies, reports on the efficacy of Nifedipine in real-life situations are more mixed, and it is not recommended that it be taken as a prophylaxis or that it be relied on as a life-saving measure in absence of other therapies.

Currency

The Tanzanian currency is the Tanzanian shilling (TZS). When I was in Tanzania in the summer of 2008, the value of the American dollar had just plunged, and the shilling was running almost even with the American dollar. Although there are a limited number of tellers in the small towns of Kilimanjaro and Moshi, guides know where to find them so that you can exchange money and pay them and their porters! You will not need any money while you're on the mountain, because, unlike the Marangu Route, the Lemosho Route does not have concession stands with items for sale. Outside of the Kilimanjaro region, it is very easy to use credit and debit cards.

---

18 Ibid.

Travel Documents

Visa

United States citizens are required to have a visa to enter Tanzania. If you are a citizen of a country other than the United States, you should check with the Tanzanian embassy to see whether you will need a visa to enter Tanzania. I did, as most travelers who travel to Tanzania do, and purchased my visa on site at the Kilimanjaro airport for $100 United States dollars (USD). You should bring enough cash to purchase your visa. Only cash is accepted. My entry was surprisingly uncomplicated.

Passport

Be sure that your passport is up to date. Your passport has to be updated every ten years. If you do not have an updated passport (meaning, one that will not expire within six months of the date of your trip), you should start the process of updating your passport at least six months prior to the anticipated date of departure. Since the September 11, 2001, terrorist attacks in the United States, it takes much longer for Americans to obtain passports. It is recommended that you give yourself a little wiggle room by starting the passport process early.

Vaccination Records

You must have a record of your vaccinations with you for inspection at the airport upon entering Tanzania. I found it easy to simply keep my vaccination record inside the holder containing my passport.

Travel and Health Insurance

I strongly suggest that you take out travel insurance for your baggage as well as for health purposes. Fortunately, I was able to take out travelers insurance with my American Express card. The travel insurance covered me in the event that my baggage was lost en route to or from Tanzania. The insurance covered the cost of replacing the items in Tanzania. This is especially important, because you will have a great deal of specialized equipment with you and in the event that it is lost, you'll need ample funds to replace the lost items, because even with travel insurance, you may not be reimbursed for lost items until you return home.

Contact your health insurance company to find out if they cover the cost of medical care abroad. Some insurance policies do not cover adventure sport and travel. It is also worth checking to see if your insurance company will pay if you are unfortunate enough to require evacuation from the mountain. Another cost is that of having to leave the country earlier than planned in order to get appropriate medical attention. Some insurance packages offer a "trip cancellation/interruption" package. This covers the cost of your airline ticket in the event that you need to leave Tanzania and return to your home country to seek medical care .

CHAPTER 7:   WHAT WILL YOU NEED DURING THE TREK?

I found it most helpful to start purchasing clothing and other items a month before the actual trip. The first thing I did was to consult the shopping list that the trekking company provided. I kept the list in my purse and consulted it whenever I went on a "Kilimanjaro shopping spree," checking off each individual item as I purchased it. I simply labeled a box "Kilimanjaro" and dropped clothing and other items into the box as I bought them. Most outfitters worth their salt will provide you with a list of suggested items to pack. My list was very comprehensive. I recommend that you not stray from the outfitter's list, and if you do, do so only to add items; not delete.

I bought everything on the list, and as it turned out, I needed everything. However, some things were more useful than others. (See table 4 for the items I took on the trek and their relative usefulness.)

Sign displayed at the trail head of the Lemosho route.

Table 4. Usefulness of Clothing and Other Items on Kilimanjaro Trek.

Items	Utility		
	Very Useful	Useful	Not Useful
Balaclava		X	
Baseball cap		X	
CamelBak pack	X		
Down jacket	X		
Down vest		X	
Fleece gloves	X		
Fleece jacket	X		
Gaiters	X		
Head lamp	X		
Lantern			X
Mittens	X		
Peek-through hat			X
Portable aqua iodine tablets	X		
Rain coat	X		
Rubber feet for walking poles			X
Shoe-liner socks			X
Sleeping bag, expedition quality	X		
Sleeping pad	X		
Steel-toe hiking boots	X		
SteinPen water purifier			X
Trekking poles	X		
Water-proof hiking pants			X
Wool, expedition-weight long underwear	X		

Be forewarned that the climbing equipment is very expensive. (See appendix A for an itemized cost of the major trekking items.) The expense is largely due to the specialized mountain gear needed. Much of the gear is tailored to specific climates and not easily bought at stores that are outside specialty shops like Recreational Equipment Incorporated (REI). REI is the Home Depot of trekking and mountaineering equipment and it is hard to find comparable prices and clothing at other places. Here I list items that, based on my experience, are critical to a successful trek.

Clothing

Perhaps one of the most daunting tasks in preparing for the Mount Kilimanjaro trek is deciding which items to take along with you and which to leave behind. Normally when you plan for a trip, you pack clothes that match the weather and activity of your destination. If you're going to the beach, you pack swimwear and plenty of shorts. If you are taking a trip during the fall, you'll likely pack a few sweaters along with moderately warm items. As you are packing clothes for your Mount Kilimanjaro trek, I suggest that you pretend that you are going to the beach, the mountains, and Antarctica, because you will need clothes for all of these climates.

The weather pattern on the mountain changes daily, so you'll find that you literally need clothing for all seasons: winter, spring, summer, fall, and rainy. I started the trek in thin hiking pants and a short-sleeved t-shirt. By the time I reached the summit, I had on an all-over snow suit and down jacket. Initially, when I heard that we would need to have clothes for different climates throughout the trip, I was obsessed over how I would determine what to put on at any given time on any day, and how I would manage to fit the clothes in my backpack. As it turns out, when you are on the mountain, you will see a marked trend in the weather each day. For instance, it will become clear when you awake whether or not the weather is going to be warm or cold, just from looking at the sky or assessing the wind pattern. This will give you some idea about the type of climate you will likely encounter during the day's trek. The trekking guide will also tell you what the weather is likely to be and the kind of clothes you should bring with you for the day. On some occasions, the weather may change during the trek and you'll need to have different clothes for the varying weather patterns. If you are prone to either becoming too hot or too cold, you may want to alter the guide's recommendation based on your own tolerance of the temperature and weather. The only clothing item that I needed and did not have was shoes to change into when I arrived at camp each night. Otherwise, I was very pleased with my preparedness with respect to my clothing.

Hiking Boots

You should put a lot of effort into finding comfortable hiking boots because if your hiking boots are uncomfortable, your trek could be dreadful. I purchased my boots at REI, and they fit perfectly. It is also a good idea to purchase your hiking boots early enough to wear them several times before your trip. After I purchased my hiking boots, I wore them often—while cutting the grass and doing various chores in my yard. I also walked long distances in them to determine how comfortable they were when I was wearing thick hiking socks. Which brings me to another point: when trying on your boots for purchase, and each time you wear them afterwards, you should have on the socks that you plan on wearing during the trek. I wore hiking boots that I had purchased years ago for a hiking trip in Costa Rica. My Costa Rica trip was more like a long walk, and my hiking boots were overkill. Not so for the Kilimanjaro trip. One feature that I particularly appreciated and would recommend is steel toes. These were very useful on parts of the trail where there was heavy brush that obstructed the view of tree roots and other items. On a couple of occasions my feet hit large tree roots, yet it was not painful because of the steel toes on my boots.

Cell Phone

I strongly encourage you to take a cell phone. If you choose to carry a cell phone, be sure to activate the international dialing feature on your phone prior to leaving the United States. It is very difficult to enable this feature once you are in Tanzania. As of July 2008, Nokia is the only cell phone company that has a tower on the mountain. Cell phones can be very useful on the mountain, especially if you are interested in keeping your family and friends informed of your progress during your climb. You should also be aware that cell phones are ubiquitous in Tanzania. Everyone has a cell phone, from the average person in the middle of cities like Arusha or Dar Es Salam to the Masai warrior out in the most remote part of Tanzania. Businesses will not allow you to use their landline telephone to make calls, local or otherwise. They are very upfront about this "no phone use" policy and even look at you askance whenever you inquire about using the phone, fully expecting you to have your own. Everyone else does. If you do not bring a cell phone, you will have to use the phone located in public phone facilities throughout Tanzania. Calls at these "telephone stations" can be very expensive. A ten-minute phone call can cost upwards of fifty U.S. dollars. Before leaving the United States, I contacted my cell phone provider and found out that the cost of a global BlackBerry PDA (Model 8830) was $ 519 USD. I decided not to purchase a BlackBerry and did not make arrangements to use my cell phone on the mountain because of the expense. However, after encountering health problems in the city and needing a cell phone to make calls to the United States, I would strongly suggest that you arrange with your cell phone provider to make international phone calls, or go ahead and bite the bullet and purchase a global Blackberry that will allow you to make phone calls as well as send email messages. It will save you a lot of hassle and may be your saving grace in the event of an emergency.

Trekking Poles

I purchased trekking poles manufactured by Leki (Teflon Super Makalu Aergon Antishock). This type of pole was recommended in one of the guide books I consulted before my trek. After milling around the aisles in REI, I decided to speak with a man who was also looking at trekking poles. He looked like the camping type, so I inquired about his recommendations. He suggested the same poles that were touted in some of the reading I had done. This corroboration was good enough for me, so I decided to go ahead and purchase the Leki brand. I must say that I was not disappointed. They worked superbly, especially when making the descent.

Head Lamp

The head lamp was incredibly useful, because there were nights when it was pitch black and rather than having to hold a flashlight, I was able to have the light perched on my head and aimed directly on to the spot where I needed it. The head lamp was also useful when I needed to find my way to the toilet in the middle of the night, find my way to the breakfast tent before dawn, and journal in the middle of the night.

Wristwatch

I recommend that you purchase a water-repellant wristwatch with a backlight and alarm. I found the alarm very useful for getting up on time. Although the guides will generally come to wake you at about 6:30 a.m., it is helpful if you have an alarm that will sound to wake you several minutes before so that you are not scrambling to pull your things together right before camp breaks each morning. The water resistance was useful during the part of the trek where we hiked through rain forest and there was a drizzly mist. Being able to see the time in the middle of the night was convenient as well.

Bug Repellant

Do not forget to take along bug repellant. This will be very useful when you begin the trek, when it is warm and sunny and mosquitoes and other insects are plentiful. Be sure to buy insect repellant that contains 25 percent to 50 percent DEET. If you use permethrin-based repellant, apply it only to your clothing, shoes, and camping gear, not directly on your skin.

Food

Most trekking companies will provide food for you while you're on the mountain. The food is provided by local cooks. Each night we looked forward to a warm meal—especially the hot soup. After partaking of such delicious food, our trekking party ceremoniously promoted our "cook" to the position of "chef." The food was prepared fresh daily and always consisted of a starch or two, meat (usually chicken or fish), hot soup or porridge, and bread. The food was outstanding and so was the meal service. Before each dinner, popcorn was served as a snack. The cook was impeccably clean, and I had no problem digesting any of the food served. We had absolutely great dishes each day we were on the mountain. At the end of a day of trekking for four to seven hours, you're usually starving and crave anything hot. As a result, meals are tastier than you could imagine. Our cook was fabulous! He was also very fastidious in his meal preparation and whipped up what appeared to be gourmet meals in the middle of nowhere. There were no complaints about the meals to be sure. Meals consisted of three courses, including soup, fruit, and a main dish of meat and vegetables. Do not expect dessert. If you must have something sweet, I would suggest bringing cookies, chocolate bars, or anything that you think you'll crave.

Although the trekking agency provides food, it is a good idea to bring some munchies to snack on while you are trekking. I'd suggest bringing trail mix. This is good for munching during the short breaks along the trek or at the campsite at night. My trekking partners brought health bars along. I chose not to take health bars, because I am not very familiar with the brands and flavors and on occasion when I have tried them I have gotten nauseous. I also carried several of the freeze-dried meals produced by the company Mountaineering. I was glad that I'd brought them along. They were good to have when I was suffering from Acute Mountain Sickness (AMS) and could only tolerate liquids. It was very easy to request hot water to prepare the dehydrated meals.

Also, it is good to bring along any specialty drinks or teas that you enjoy as well as your specific brand of coffee. The coffee provided by the trekking company was an instant blend that was extremely weak. Quite frankly, it was awful. I was glad that I'd taken the advice of other climbers and brought my own container of Folgers coffee. It made the mornings of the trek much better! It was apparently very noticeable that I was avoiding the instant coffee offered by the server. After seeing me drinking my Folger's coffee on three consecutive mornings, he took my large jar of Folgers coffee and packed it along with the cook's other items and began placing it on the table when breakfast was served. From this point on, my Folgers coffee was served throughout the trek. I forgot to bring my very own hot chocolate, and oh how I missed it! The hot chocolate the company served was worse than the coffee. On the one day that I drank the hot chocolate, I was sick the very next morning. It could have been just a coincidence, but I never drank any more hot chocolate the rest of the trip.

Be mindful that the higher you are up on the mountain, the less sanitary are the conditions. As you ascend with the group, be very cautious about eating leftover food and be very conscious of dishes washed in communal pails.

Toiletries

Another item of concern is toiletries. Ah, the joy of toilet paper! The first thing that you'll hear from every traveler is to bring your own toilet paper. Although the porters have toilet paper, it can be quite humiliating to have to go to the guide or porter every time you want to wipe your butt. Bring your own toilet paper. You should also bring bar soap as well as hand soap. Hand wipes are also a good item to have. I brought over fifty individually wrapped hand wipes and still ran out near the end of the trip. Fortunately, I also had hand wipes that were packaged in a plastic container. Sanitation is a premium and indeed by the end of the trip you will feel as if you could sit in a tub and soak for days. Depending on your age and menopausal status, you may need to bring other sanitary supplies, such as tampons and sanitary napkins, as well as plastic bags for their disposal.

First-Aid Kit

You never know when you'll have a medical emergency on the mountain. So it is a good idea to bring a first-aid kit so that you can handle minor emergencies, like a small cut or scrape, for which you'll need bandages and antiseptics. A list of items to be included in your first aid kit is in appendix D. My first-aid kit came in handy when I needed bandages for my toe that was badly blistered and bruised because it kept rubbing against the front of my steel-toe boots as I was descending the mountain. I later found out that my socks were too thick for the descent! I should have had on my thinner socks when going *down* the mountain. This is something you might want to keep in mind.

Plastic Bags

You should bring along a few extra-large plastic bags to store your waste for discarding in trash bins in designated areas or when you leave the mountain. REI sells oversized plastic bags that are especially manufactured to mask smell, and you will not have a foul odor coming out of your duffle bag or day pack. I used several while on the mountain and found them to be excellent at containing the odor of the salmon I took with me for protein during the hike. You can also use the bags to store used toilet paper and feminine hygiene products. Given the focus on environmental stewardship—which emphasizes the "leave no trace" ethics—you would be wise to use "waste bags." If you do not properly dispose of your waste, people will notice and will not hesitate to scold you.

Cash for Tipping

Bring enough cash to tip the porters and guides generously. I am sure that, like others before you, you will not be disappointed with the porters' assistance throughout the trek. People often rant and rave about the porters and their ability to carry heavy items while traversing the mountain to the very top while the poor novice mountain climbers fight for every breath, carrying only a backpack. My trekking partner had envelopes with the name of each porter written on the outside. This made it very easy to distribute their tips at the end of the trek. I highly recommend that you do the same. While I was struggling to count out the Tanzania currency to be sure that I was tipping each porter appropriately, my fellow trekking partners simply distributed pre-labeled envelopes to each porter. I spent roughly seven hundred dollars in tips. We had fifteen porters for three women in my expedition. In order to split the cost and tip each porter fairly, we decided that each of us would tip five porters each. We all gave the porters the same amount: $7 per day. We tipped the guides individually. I gave both guides $15 dollars per day each. Each of us tipped the cook. I do not know how much others in my trekking party gave the cook (a.k.a. "Chef"). I gave the chef $10 per day.

Sunglasses

Prior to my trip, I had never paid more than twenty dollars for sunglasses. I spent $80 on a discount pair of sunglasses for the trek and felt that it was money well spent. For ample protection, purchase sunglasses with 100 percent UV blocking.

Backpack/Rucksack

I purchased a CamelBak hydration pack, which is a backpack that has a special storage space for water and tubing that extends outside the bag and close to your mouth for easy access for drinking water. I highly recommend you purchase a CamelBak, as it will enable you to stay constantly hydrated. I would also suggest buying a CamelBak with ample room for storage. All the little pockets and hidden storage space made a big difference in what I was able to take with me during the day.

Sunscreen

Having dark skin, I never routinely use sunscreen. However, just before leaving Atlanta, my boyfriend, who is European-American and has very fair skin that burns easily, insisted that I take sunscreen, so we stopped by the local drug store and I bought a bottle of sunscreen and packed it among my other belongings. This urging turned out to be very sound. Even if you have dark skin, I want to emphasize the need to take and apply sunscreen. I assumed that I would not get sunburned because I have rather dark skin and have never sustained sunburn during my entire life, but I was wrong. I only used a minimal amount of sunscreen, even as we ascended very close to the top of the mountain. After the trek, it was rather amusing that even though I had the darkest skin (by far), I was the only one with severe sunburn! I now know what it feels like to be sunburned, and it is not pleasant. Sunburn on the mountain can be dangerous, as it can affect your body's ability to cool itself and leads to a loss of body fluids. It is recommended that you use sunscreen of SPF 15 or higher. The most effective products say "broad spectrum" or "UVA/UVB protection" on their labels. Don't forget to apply the sunscreen liberally and often.

Journal and Writing Utensils

The ink ran out in my pen and I did not have an extra pen. I was able to borrow a pen from a park ranger who happened to be on the mountain. Pencils and pens are surprisingly hard to find in the city of Arusha, let alone on the mountain. So if you plan to write in your journal, I suggest you take several writing utensils.

Whistle

A whistle may come in handy if you get separated from your trekking party and need to let someone know your location on the mountain. It may also come in handy if you want to alert someone in the event that you are in imminent danger for some reason.

Polychlorinated Biphenyl (PCB)-Free Nalgene Bottles

These bottles are very handy for transporting extra water. What worked well for me was to fill the bottles with water (32 ounces) and drop water purification tablets in the water. This allowed me to follow the directions for the purification tablets easily, which called for 1 tablet per 32 ounces of water. After the tablets were mixed in the water and had sat for the specified period of time, I poured the purified water into my CamelBak. By doing this, I was always assured that the water I was drinking was sufficiently purified. I also used the bottles as foot warmers. On really cold nights, the porters would fill the bottles with boiling hot water and I would place the warm bottles in my sleeping bag—usually near my feet. This made the nights inside the sleeping bag nice and toasty.

Sleeping Bag

I purchased a Marmot CWM EQ-40 sleeping bag designed for extreme cold (-40 degrees Fahrenheit), high-altitude mountaineering. This was the one item among all the specialized mountain gear that I truly appreciated on the eve of the summit attempt. Although it was well below freezing, I was warm and cozy inside my sleeping bag.

CHAPTER 8: MATERIALS AND BOOKS TO READ BEFORE AND AFTER YOUR KILIMANJARO TREK

While searching the Web site *Amazon.com*, I found more than four hundred books on Mount Kilimanjaro. To help focus my reading, I decided to read books that would help me accomplish the following objectives:

- Assist me in the physical preparation for the trek
- Provide me with first-hand accounts that would help me get a sense of what I would encounter during the climb
- Provide me with facts on acclimatization and the history of Mount Kilimanjaro

I also purposely chose not to read books that I thought might discourage me from taking the climb or those that I might better appreciate after climbing Mount Kilimanjaro. Listed below are books and materials that I read or consulted both before and after trekking Mount Kilimanjaro.

Books I Read before Trekking

Benjamin, M. 2005. *Swahili Phrasebook*. Oakland: Lonely Planet Publications.

Berzucka, S. 2005. *Altitude Illness: Prevention and Treatment (Mountaineers' Outdoor Expert)*. Seattle: The Mountaineers Books.

Brashears, D. 2002. *Kilimanjaro: To the Roof of Africa*. DVD.

Carmichael, S. and Stoddard, S. 2002. *Climbing Mount Kilimanjaro* (2nd ed.). Lansing: Medi-Ed Press.

Gray, P. 2006. *Kilimanjaro via the Marangu Route: "Tourist Route" My Ass*. Lincoln: iUniverse.

Green, D. 2005. *Uhuru Peak: The Quest for Mt. Kilimanjaro* United States: Instantpublisher.com.

International Travel Maps: Kilimanjaro (3rd ed.). 2007. Vancouver: ITMB Publishing, LTD.

Megarry, J. 2002. *Explore Mount Kilimanjaro: Marangu, Macame, and Rongai Routes*. UK: Rucksack Readers.

Poindexter, J. 1998. *To Summit: Fifty Mountains that Lure, Inspire, and Challenge*. New York: Black Dog and Leventhal Publishers.

Stedman, H. 2006 *Kilimanjaro: The Trekking Guide to Africa's Highest Mountain* (2nd ed.). Surry, UK: Trailblazer Publications.

Books I Read after Trekking:

Bowling, J.C. 2007. Making the Climb: What a Novice Climber Learned about Life on Mount Kilimanjaro. Kansas City: Beacon Hill Press.

Krakauer, J. 1997. Into Thin Air: A Personal Account of the Mt. Everest disaster. New York: Anchor Books, a division of Random House.

Krakauer, J. 1996. Into The Wild. New York: Anchor Books, a division of Random House.

Sawaya, A. 2005. Kilimanjaro with Passion. Victoria, BC: Trafford Publishing.

Simpson, J. 1998. Touching the Void: The true Story of One Man's Miraculous Survival. New York, NY: Harper Collins Publishers Inc.

CHAPTER 9: MY REFLECTIONS

So what did I learn during my solo trek up the mountain? The first lesson I learned was one I never sought but which came to me at the right time: I am much stronger than I thought. Second, I realized that in order to fight the self-doubt, depression, and remorse that had chased me for years, I need to keep moving and stay focused. It was only when I was in motion that my sense of self-importance vanished. With the disappearance of self-importance came the vanishing of self-doubt, depression, and regret. This lesson was learned during a moment of excruciating fatigue while trying to ascend to an altitude of 17,500 feet. I was miserably sick and wondered whether I could or should keep going. As I was fighting the urge to vomit and trying to keep my bearings despite the toll mountain sickness was having on me, I realized that I needed to stay completely focused on the task at hand: reaching the summit. That meant that I needed to avoid distractions of any kind, both mental and physical. I constantly avoided thinking about the negative comments of others: "Are you sure you want to do this?" "Let us pray for you, just in case you do not come back," and "I'm just afraid that rather than die, you'll go into a coma and never wake up."

While perched on the ledge of a boulder on the Western Breach, the toughest part of the climb, these negative thoughts began swirling around in my head. I dismissed them as soon as they entered my mind and replaced them with one single thought: "The race does not go to the fastest or swiftest but to him who endures." I remembered this phrase from somewhere in the Bible, and it seemed a fitting mantra for the occasion. I recited this phrase over and over in my head. I noticed that when I looked to either side, I saw precipitous drops. Each time I looked anywhere other than straight ahead, I became queasy. So I stopped looking to the sides and began to look straight ahead. In fact, I began to look only at the step I was taking. Nothing was more important to me than the step immediately ahead. I began only to think about the task before me. I became so tired that I could not eat. I could barely drink water, but I stayed focused.

Even on the trek, it was the men who provided for me materially and kept me out of harm's way, while the women offered refuge through their late-night conversations, cajoling, and small talk. I learned that that's okay! After trekking through the forest all day, I would lay beneath the moon staring at the stars, hoping for an answer to that important question: What do I want out of life? I discovered that I wanted very little. I want the intangible: love and meaningful social interaction. I began to appreciate what it meant to have someone with you with an outstretched hand in the deepest, toughest hours. I felt what it is like to be totally vulnerable to place and time.

What did I think about my preparation for journeying through life without a lifelong partner? Well, I learned that I am still not comfortable being completely alone. While I enjoyed the solitary experience, afterwards, I realized that the adjustment to being alone was as steep as the mountain itself. This was painfully clear whenever I became caught up in my own little world, applauding myself for not feeling alone and feeling empowered. Then, as I was headed down the mountain, all alone—even the assistant guide, seeing that I was only yards from the end of the trail, had abandoned me—I suddenly heard someone yelling. It was the young man whom I had walked past right after I had left the summit. He yelled out, "You're alone again? Every time I see you, you're alone." At that moment, I remembered that I was indeed alone. The reality set in, and I felt lonely. I realized that, although I needed to be alone, I didn't necessarily want to be alone. At that moment, I wondered why I had not fallen to my death when my hand slipped from a rock at 17,500 feet. I also wondered why the very people who did all of the work got so little credit. It was at the point that I asked myself again: Did I do the best thing for my ailing mother? Did I make the wrong decisions regarding her care? Did those decisions cut short rather than prolong her life? I asked these questions at several points on the journey. Each time I asked I would pause, fully expecting that I would get an answer. There were no answers. I learned that there are questions in life that will never be answered, and that there are answers that will never be understood.

REFERENCES

Bezruchka, Stephen. 2005. *Altitude Illness: Prevention and Treatment (Mountaineers Outdoor Expert)*, 2nd ed. Seattle: The Mountaineers Books.

Carmichael, Stephen and Susan Stoddard. 2002. Climbing Mount Kilimanjaro, 2nd ed. Michigan: Medi-Ed Press.

Poindexter, Joseph. 1998. *To the Summit: Fifty Mountains that Lure, Inspire, and Challenge.* New York: Black Dog and Leventhal Publishers.

Stedman, Henry. 2006. *Kilimanjaro: The Trekking Guide to Africa's Highest Mountain.* 2nd ed. Surrey, UK: Trailblazer Publications.

Appendix A.
Itemized Trek Expenses

Item	Cost
Kilisummit Trekking Company	3,183
Airline tickets	2,266
Clothing*	1,000
Porter tips	700
Marmot Col EQ sleeping bag-regular	679
Lodging (Ngurdoto Mountain Lodge)	568
Medical expenses**	220
Leki Super Makai trekking poles	150
Travel insurance	102
CamelBak pack	100
REI Lite Core, 1.5 sleeping pad	75
Petzl Tikka Plus LED headlamp	40
Portable aqua iodine tablets (2 bottles)	20
GRAND TOTAL*	**9,103**

* Conservative estimate

** Includes immunizations, prescription drugs and travel clinic visits. Prescription drugs covered by my medical insurance plan are not included in this cost.

***Costs are rounded to the nearest dollar; based on 2008 prices, and do not include food, incidentals, and snacks consumed while trekking.

Appendix B. Actual Page from Diary Kept on the Mountain*

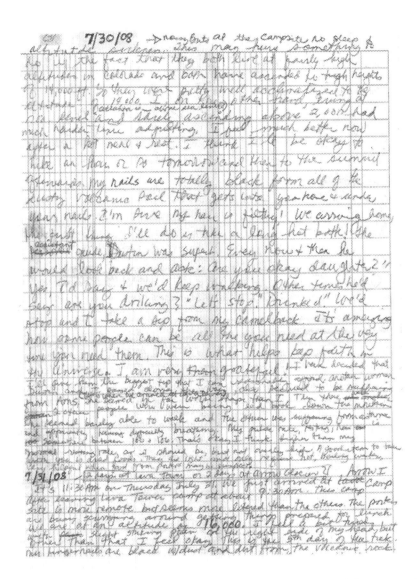

*My notes were written on drafting paper that I borrowed from a park ranger because I mistakenly left my journal at the lodge.

Appendix C. Food Log

DAY	BREAKFAST	LUNCH	DINNER	SNACK	EXERCISE	Water Intake
Mon 5/7	1 cup of coffee 1 apple 1 strawberry crepe with yogurt and walnuts	Salmon and Pasta left over from restaurant (note: quite a bit of olive oil)	1 piece of salmon (not sure of weight); stir-fried potato (1 small potato) and tossed salad with drizzle of drsg.	1 orange	30 mins treadmill 15 mins bicycle	Little water –very little. Drank black tea
Tues 5/8	1 cup of coffee 1 apple	Chicken strips and salad greens (8-10 strips) 1 slice of pineapple	Tossed salad w/0 drsg; 2 large serving spoons of rice w/ broccoli, mushrooms and ½ piece of salmon	1 small piece of Hershey chocolate	30 mins treadmill 25 mins bicycle	Drinking water thr. out the day

89

Weds. 5/9	1 apple 1 cup of coffee 1 kiwi	Salmon and rice w/broccoli, mushrooms, onions	Grouper sandwich (w/0 bread) and 1 tsp of gumbo soup, 10 french fries	1 orange 1 bag of popcorn 1 box of hard candy	none	Drinking water all day
Thurs. 5/10	1 cup of coffee 1 cup of black tea	Tossed spinach salad w/ light no-fat drsg and salmon 1 cup of soup	Rice and chicken stir fry w/ tomato sauce, tomatoes, onion, mushroom, and green beans	1 small piece of Hershey chocolate candy	none	Drinking water part of day
Fri 5/11	1 cup of hot chocolate (made from cocoa and splenda) 1 apple 6 strawberries	Turkey wrap and a teaspoon of rice and turkey-mixture leftover from dinner Baked chips	Salmon salad with 3 breaded shrimp	1 orange	1 hour jogging	1 bottle of water (20 fl ounces)

Sat 5/12	1 cup of coffee	½ chicken sandwich from Chick-fil-A, French fries and spoonful of chicken strip with Cajun rice	Chili's restaurant: ½ rack of ribs Side tossed salad w/o salad drsg. French fries ½ brownie w/ ice cream, fudge and caramel syrup	none	1 hour jogging	Less than the preferred amount
Sun 5/13	1 cup of coffee	4 baked chicken wings Rice stir-fry White rice	Salmon salad ¼ rack of ribs (shared with Tom)	shared slice of chocolate cake and fresh strawberries with Tom	1 hour jogging	Less than the preferred amount

Appendix D. Items to Include in First Aid Kit[19]

Medical Supplies	Use
Adhesive tape	used for holding gauze to the skin
Bandages	used in splints to support broken bones
Elastic support bandage	used to support sprained knees or ankles
Gauze swabs	used for dressing a wound
Non-adhesive dressings	used for dressing a wound
Safety pins	may be used for holding bandages together
Small pair of scissors	used for cutting the gauze into smaller pieces
Sterile alcohol wipes	used to clean the wound
Steri-strips	protects the wound from infection
Sutures	used to close an open wound
Syringes and needles	used for giving medication intravenously
Thermometer	needed for checking your temperature
Tweezers	removal of splinters embedded in the skin
Acetaminophen (Tylenol)	headache, pain killer, fever
Acetazolamide (Diamox)	speed acclimatization, treat mild AMS
Antibiotic cream	for application to infected wounds
Betadine solution	for minor cuts and abrasions
Codeine	painkiller and cough suppressant
Dexamethasone (Decadron)	severe AMS or HACE
Diphenhydramine	allergies and sleep
Ibuprofen	headache, muscle aches and pain, frostbite and sunburn
Immodium	diarrhea
Lablosan	lip protection
Metronidazole or Trinidazole	anitbiotic
Oral rehydration salts	for treatment of severe diarrhea
Promethazine	nausea, vomiting
Sun Block	sunburn prevention
Throat Lozenges	sore throat

19 ABC-of-Mountaineering, "First Aid and Medical Kits", http://www.abc-of-mountaineering.com/articles/medical.asp.